DIVINE ENGINEERING

Scriptural Accounts and Scientific Truths about the Earth's Creation Are Compatible

David N. Brems

Springville, Utah

ISBN: 1-55517-683-6
e.1

Published by Cedar Fort, Inc.
www.cedarfort.com

Distributed by:

Cover design by Nicole Cunningham

Printed in the United States of America
10 9 8 7 6 5 4 3 2 1

Printed on acid-free paper

Library of Congress Cataloging-in-Publication Data

Brems, David N.
Divine engineering : Scriptural accounts and scientific truths about the earth's creation are compatible / David N. Brems.
p. cm.
Includes bibliographical references (p.).
ISBN 1-55517-683-6
1. Creation. 2. Church of Jesus Christ of Latter-day Saints--Doctrines. I. Title.
BX8643.C75B74 2003
231.7'65--dc21

2002156579

Contents

Chapter 1

Introduction

A few years ago I received a desperate phone call from one of the young women of our ward. "Brother Brems, I am so confused! In my high school science class I am learning about the big bang theory, evolution, the ancient age of the earth, cavemen, and dinosaurs. How can all this be compatible with the gospel and the scriptural accounts of the creation?" I told her that I had spent over thirty years of my adult life trying to sort out the revelations of God with respect to the facts deduced from science. After several follow-up conversations with her I could sense her confusion levels fading and her confidence in the scriptures growing. I wondered why we leave our young people so disarmed relative to modern science and the creation. Since that time and whenever possible I have tried to erase this unnecessary confusion between science and the gospel. There is absolutely no need for students of the gospel and of science to feel as though they must choose one or the other.

Reason suggests that truth should be consistent whether revealed by God or deduced by logic from the laboratory. Albert Einstein, a religious man according to his own definition, said it well: "Science without religion is lame and religion without science is blind" (Einstein, 1956). Doctrine and Covenants 88:40 commands us to embrace truth, and 93:36 says that, "the glory of God is intelligence, or . . . light and truth." There is little doubt that real truth will be highly consistent and compatible regardless of its source. One of my personal heroes, my instructor in physical chemistry, the late Henry Eyring said, "Science has rendered a service to religion. The scientific spirit is a spirit of inquiry, a spirit of reaching out for truth. In the final analysis, this spirit is the essence of religion" (Eyring, 1983). The Savior said, "Ask, and it shall be given you; seek, and ye shall find; knock, and it shall be opened unto you" (Matt. 7:7). Throughout this book the scriptures are liberally interpreted in the light of modern scientific evidence. Through the spectacles of science, the horizon of scriptural interpretation is magnified and new vistas will be envisioned.

An axiom running throughout this book is that God is the ultimate scientist and created the earth through the mastery and use of the eternal laws and principles of physics and chemistry. Many remnants of the creation were left behind for the modern-day creation seeker. The creation was accomplished through obedience to fundamental principles and as a result the remnants are sometimes incorrectly interpreted in a Godless fashion. My goal in writing this book is to share with others whatever insight I may have gained from this lifelong search. My own testimony regarding the divine nature of the creation has been fortified and enhanced by this process. If others benefit even a fraction of what I have gained, then my effort has been worth every minute. The theme throughout this book is that the scriptures are of divine origin and are interpreted in a manner consistent with the best scientific truth. In other words, the scriptures are explained in light of the truth from science and vice versa. The Doctrine and Covenants, in section 88 verses 78–79, admonishes, "Teach ye diligently . . . that you may be instructed more perfectly in theory, in principle, in doctrine . . . in all things . . . Of things both in heaven and in the earth, and under the earth; things which have been, things which are."

Members of the Church of Jesus Christ of Latter-day Saints are richly blessed due to their faith in additional scripture and continual revelation through modern day prophets. Regarding the creation, the Lord has revealed three versions that we will consider in detail; the Biblical version from Genesis and the two versions from the Pearl of Great Price, from the books of Moses and Abraham. The prophet Joseph Smith received additional revelations concerning the creation and the universe that are recorded in the Doctrine and Covenants. All these versions of the creation are very similar but important and subtle differences are apparent. These differences provide profound insight into the creation, particularly with respect to the truth from modern science. By providing modern humans with three versions of the creation, the Lord emphasizes the similarities through repetition and also adds new insight for Latter-day Saints. The repeated messages from all the scriptural versions of the creation are; it occurred step-by-step, it started with the simplest and proceeded to the more complex, and God was directly involved. The subtle differences between the scriptural versions and additional latter-day revelation emphasize the creation was a carefully planned process, the ancient age of the earth, and the involvement of multiple Gods. An important adjustment in thinking for some readers will be the willingness to accept the reality of the ancient age of the earth. The scriptures, particularly those revealed and translated through the prophet Joseph Smith, provide ample evidence for a scriptural foundation for the ancient age of the earth.

God considers the creation story vital to his earthly children. The doctrine of the creation is fundamental to and lays a proper foundation for all other doctrine of the gospel. For this reason He has provided us with three separate scriptural versions. The very first message of the Bible is the creation. Appreciating God's direct involvement and the painstaking effort required to create the earth is essential to our worship. A loving God prepared a beautiful, resource-abundant, and replenishing earth as a home for his spirit children to dwell on while they worked out the critical steps of their exaltation.. The greater our understanding, the stronger will be our faith and worship. To understand the role of the Savior as the Creator helps us to better know Him and enhances our relationship with Him. The temples of the Lord have been established for us to receive further light, knowledge, and the endowment. The ultimate blessings of the temple are richly embedded in the creation story.

The hope and prayer of this author is that the reader will consider the information that follows with an open mind and truth-seeking attitude. By doing so, the agreement between the revealed word of God and the truths discovered through scientific investigation will become apparent.

2

Comparison of Scriptural Truths: Days 1 and 2

The first two days of the Creation were focused on the initial formation of the earth, the sun, and the early atmosphere, referred to as firmament or expanse, which contained considerable water vapor. The account in Moses clearly teaches of the role of the Savior in the creation. Abraham instructs us further of the involvement of multiple Gods and their plurality. Abraham provides insight regarding the eternal nature of the elements and uses terminology such as "organized" that is consistent with the first law of thermodynamics from modern science. Abraham gives us the first clues that a "creation day" was not a twenty-four-hour period but rather an extended length of time by using the phrase "brooding" and referring to the second creation "time" rather than using day.

Latter-day Saints have additional insight into the creation. Besides Genesis we have two additional revelations that are contained in the Pearl of Great Price—the books of Moses and Abraham. Both Genesis and the Book of Moses are revelations believed to have been delivered to the prophet Moses (Skousen, 1953). The Book of Abraham is a revelation given to Abraham that, along with the Book of Moses, was made available through translations by the prophet Joseph Smith. The repetition of three accounts of the creation must represent the emphasis and importance of this event. Comparison of the three versions results in the striking conclusion that they are very similar.

The similarity of the accounts is a strong witness to the accuracy of the translations, emphasizes the consistency, and validates the creation story. However, there are subtle differences between the accounts that shed new and interesting light on the creation. In this chapter we will compare and contrast each verse from the three recordings pertaining to creation days one and two. An additional account of the creation has been revealed to the Prophet Joseph Smith and is only available to those that attend the temple. The similarities are overwhelming for the description revealed in the temple to those of scriptural origin. Like the other accounts, new insights are made available through the temple version. Careful listening and attention through repeated temple attendance will reveal new horizons. Due to the sacredness and sanctity of the temple, any additional comments and reference to the creation story as shared in the temple will not be described or discussed.

Genesis	**Moses**	**Abraham**
1. In the beginning God created the heaven and the earth.	1. . . . by mine Only Begotten I created these things: yea, in the beginning I created the heaven and the earth upon which thou standest.	1. . . . and they, that is the Gods, organized and formed the heavens and the earth.

The first verse of the Moses account emphasizes the critical role of the Savior, the Only Begotten, in the creation process. This is an important distinction that is not clearly portrayed in the Genesis description. Doctrine and Covenants 76:24 further reveals, "That by him, through him, and of him the worlds are and were created." The work was directed by Elohim and by his power, but the Son performed the actual work. This explains why Christ is referred to as the Creator of this world. Doctrine and Covenants 38:3 says, referring to Christ, "I am the same which spake, and the world was made, and all things came by me." A very important principle was revealed in Doctrine and Covenants 76:24 and in Moses 7:30—that Christ created "millions of earths like this." Thus, Christ is the creator of worlds without number.

Abraham adds further insight by specifically using the plural form, Gods. We can conclude from Abraham that multiple Gods were involved. In 1820 the prophet Joseph Smith was visited by two distinct divine personages, God the Father (Elohim) and Jesus Christ his Son. Thus, at least two Gods, the Father and Son were involved in the creation. The plural usage of Gods by Abraham is explained in 3:22–24. Many of the noble and great ones were with Christ. Abraham wrote, " . . . and he said unto those who were with him: We will go down, for there is space there, and we will take of these materials, and we will make an earth whereon these may dwell." The latter-day prophet Joseph Fielding Smith taught that these noble ones included Michael (Adam), Enoch, Noah, Abraham, Moses, Peter, James, and John, Joseph Smith, and many others (Smith, 1954, 74–75).

Abraham provides additional insight by the use of the verb "organized" rather than "created" as used in Genesis and Moses. "Organized" emphasizes taking existing matter and rearranging it to make the earth.

Joseph Smith, in a sermon at the funeral of his friend King Follett in 1844, said: "You ask the learned doctors why they say the world was made out of nothing; and they will answer, Doesn't the Bible say He created the world? And they infer, from the word create, that it must have been made out of nothing. Now, the word create came from the word *baurau*, which does not mean to create out of nothing; it means to organize; the same as a man would organize materials and build a ship. Hence we infer that God had materials to organize the world out of chaos-chaotic matter, which is element, and in which dwells all the glory. Element had an existence from the time he had. The pure principles of element are principles that can never be destroyed; they may be organized and reorganized, but not destroyed. They had no beginning, and can have no end" (Smith, 1972, 342–62).

These teachings from the Prophet Joseph Smith showed remarkable insight considering the era. During the early to mid-1800s, science was discovering what has become known as the first law of thermodynamics, or the law of conservation of energy, which states that matter can neither be created nor destroyed, but only change form. Benjamin Thompson, Julius Robert Mayer, James Prescott Joule, and others were establishing the conservation of energy as a principle of universal validity and as one of the fundamental laws applicable to all natural phenomena. Simultaneously, John Dalton was carrying on experiments identifying that all matter was composed of fundamental elements and the atomic theory. These concepts were scientifically radical and not well accepted by all the scientific community. The prevailing theory was that of spontaneous creation and loss of matter. Joseph Smith taught the first law of thermodynamics prior to it being fully accepted by modern science and long before recognition by the common people. This is most amazing considering that Joseph Smith had no more than a third grade formal education. The hand of the Lord, the greatest of all scientists, taught Joseph Smith. Clearly Joseph Smith was a Seer and Prophet. How else could he have taught such forward-looking principles?

Genesis	**Moses**	**Abraham**
2. And the earth was without form, and void; and darkness was upon the face of the deep. And the Spirit of God moved upon the face of the waters.	2. And the earth was without form, and void; and I caused darkness to come up upon the face of the deep; and my Spirit moved upon the face of the water; for I am God.	2. And the earth, after it was formed, was empty and desolate, because they had not formed anything but the earth; and darkness reigned upon the face of the deep, and the

spirit of the Gods was brooding upon the face of the waters.

In verse 2, the Genesis and Moses accounts state that "the earth was without form." Why the earth had no "form" after its initial creation seems confusing. Abraham clarifies this situation by substituting "form" for the past tense "formed." This provides a completely different perspective and switches the emphasis to the concept that once formed the earth was void, empty, and desolate.

The use of the term "brooding" by Abraham in verse 2 connotes additional discernment. Brooding infers getting ready to parent, incubate, or hatch. This terminology suggests the passage of time and the initiation of processes that were maturing. As described in chapter 9 this is wholly consistent with modern scientific findings.

Genesis	**Moses**	**Abraham**
3. And God said, Let there be light: and there was light.	3. And I God, said: Let there be light: and there was light.	3. And they (the Gods) said: Let there be light; and there was light.

The three versions of verse 3 are very similar, except for the repeated emphasis by Abraham of the plurality of Gods involved in the creation. Verse 3 provides contrast to the description in verse 2. Verse 3 emphasizes that light appeared as a result of the Gods direct command, “And they said: Let there be light; and there was light.” Whereas, verse 2 infers that the Gods initiated processes that were brooding or incubating over time. Such examples suggest that some phases of the creation occurred instantaneously, while others transpired over time. This concept is very consistent with the scientific record that shows cataclysmic changes in addition to slow changes over time.

Genesis	Moses	Abraham
4. And God saw the light, that it was good: and God divided the light from the darkness.	4. And I, God, saw the light; and that light was good. And I, God, divided the light from the darkness.	4. And they (the Gods) comprehended the light, for it was bright; and they divided the light, or caused it to be divided, from the darkness.
5. And God called the light Day and the darkness he called Night. And the evening and the morn-ing were the first day.	5. And I, God, called the light Day; and the darkness, I called night; and this I did by the word of my power, and it was done as	5. And the Gods called the light Day, and the darkness they called Night. And it came to pass that from the evening until

	I spake; and the evening and the morning were the first day.	morning they called night; and from the morning until the evening they called day; and this was the first, or the beginning, of that which they called day and night.
6. And God said, Let there be a firmament in the midst of the waters, and let it divide the waters from the waters.	6. And again, I, God, said: Let there be a firmament in the midst of the water, and it was so, even as I spake: and I said: Let it divide the waters from the waters; and it was done;	6. And the Gods also said: Let there be an expanse in the midst of the waters, and it shall divide the waters from the waters.
7. And God made the firmament, and divided the waters which were under the firmament from the waters which were above the firmament: and it was so.	7. And I, God, made the firmament and divided the waters, yea, the great waters under the firmament from the waters which were above the firmament, and	7. And the Gods ordered the expanse, so that it divided the waters which were under the expanse from the waters which were above the expanse; and it

	it was so even as I spake.	was so, even as they ordered.
8. And God called the firmament heaven. And the evening and the morning were the second day.	8. And I, God, called the firmament Heaven; and the evening and the morning were the second day.	8. And the Gods called the expanse, Heaven. And it came to pass that it was from evening until morning that they called night; and it came to pass that it was from morning until evening that they called day; and this was the second time that they called night and day.

The Abraham version near the end of verse 8 uses the term “second time” to refer to the second period of the creation. This emphasizes and highlights that the term “days” as used in Moses and Genesis should not be strictly interpreted as a twenty-four-hour period of time. Inference by Abraham to the second creation period as a “time” lends credence to the theory that each day may have extended for long periods. Doctrine and

Covenants 130:4 instructs us that the reckoning of time is dependent on the planet, with each having its own reckoning. A possible and reasonable interpretation of Abraham's distinct use of the term "time" indicates a nonspecific period sufficient to complete the necessary work. A period of time could be variable depending on its context and reference. If necessary, it may even represent very extended periods of time, even millions of years. Each of the different periods of time may have had a different duration. This use of time by Abraham adds significant insight into the scriptural description of the creation and is consistent with the time frame elucidated by modern science.

Chapter Three

Comparison of Scriptural Truths: Day 3

Day three of the Creation is centered on formation of the oceans and dry land, and the bringing forth of plant life. Abraham reveals a most important concept with the statement, "Let us prepare the earth to bring forth" plant life. Scientific evidence indicates that much preparation was necessary for the newly formed earth to support vegetation. First, the water that was predominantly in the atmospheric vapor-state needed to condense upon the surface to form oceans. This resulted in an atmosphere more transparent to sunlight that was necessary for photosynthesis, the chief life-support process for harnessing the energy of sunlight. Plant life first appeared as single-celled organisms exclusively in the oceans. With time, more complex forms of aquatic plant life were introduced. Through the long extended process of weathering, the earth's crust was gradually broken down to fine particles that formed a primitive soil to succor plant life. The invasion of land by plants was accompanied by challenges. One strategy utilized by the Gods for the land plants was the "bringing forth of the . . . seed." In the absence of a water medium, the seed allows the young plant embryo to remain dormant and protected until favorable conditions for germination. The descriptive "preparation" phase mentioned by Abraham reflects a step-by-step process that occurred over time and is nicely consistent with the scientific scenario.

Genesis	**Moses**	**Abraham**
9. And God said, Let the waters under the heaven be gathered together unto one place, and let the dry land appear: and it was so.	9. And I, God, said: Let the waters under the heaven be gathered together unto one place, and it was so; and I, God, said: let there be dry land; and it was so.	9. And the Gods ordered, saying: Let the waters under the heaven be gathered together unto one place, and let the earth come up dry; and it was so as they ordered;
10. and God called the dry land Earth; and the gathering together of the waters called he Seas:	10. And I, God, called the dry land Earth; and the gathering together of the waters, called I the	10. And the Gods pronounced the dry land, Earth; and the gathering together of the

and God saw that it was good.

11. And God said, Let the earth bring forth grass, the herb yielding seed, and the fruit tree yielding fruit after his kind, whose seed is in itself, upon the earth: and it was so.

Sea; and I, God, saw that all things which I had made were good.

11. And I, God, said: Let the earth bring forth grass, the herb yielding seed, the fruit tree yielding fruit, after his kind, and the tree yielding fruit, whose seed should be in itself upon the earth, and it was so even as I spake.

pronounced they, Great Waters; and the Gods saw that they were obeyed.

11. And the Gods said: Let us prepare the earth to bring forth grass; the herb yielding seed; the fruit tree yielding fruit, after his kind, whose seed in itself yieldeth its own likeness upon the earth; and it was so, even as they ordered.

Prior to the bringing forth of life, Abraham, in the first portion of verse 11, adds the concept, “Let us prepare the earth.” The emphasis of preparation is significant. Preparation signifies the requirement for time and step-by-step processes. The newly created earth was full of potential, but was far from being able to support the necessary life that the Gods had planned for. The earth needed to be made ready before the advent of life. All indications from modern paleoecology suggest that the primitive earth's atmosphere and crust needed considerable preparation before life could be supported. Life as we know it today is a complex, delicate, and balanced relationship between all living organisms. For example, there is a cyclic exchange of materials and energy between living things and the environment. Numerous critical life-supporting cycles are known such as, gas/atmospheric cycle, water cycle, carbon cycle, nitrogen cycle, phosphorus cycle, and energy cycle (see Chapter Four for a discussion on these cycles and their critical interdependencies).

Preparation of the Atmosphere for Life

The early atmosphere was composed chiefly of methane (CH_4) and minor components of ammonia (NH_4), hydrogen, nitrogen, and water vapor (H_2O). This combination of gases would not sustain any form of life that we are aware of. As the interior of the earth assumed its present structure, methane and ammonia were broken down to release carbon dioxide (CO_2), hydrogen, and nitrogen gases into the atmosphere. This combination of gases would not support animal life but was ripe for plants. Plants have the unique capability to capture the ultimate energy source, sunlight, to split water molecules, produce oxygen, and synthesize energy rich compounds in an important chemical process known as photosynthesis. Plants are known as autotrophs, or self-feeders, because they don't consume other living organisms as an energy source (modern forms of animal-eating plants are exempt). The living organisms in our current ecosystem can be divided into three groups—producers, consumers and decomposers. Plants are the ultimate producer organisms on earth, they take the energy of sunlight to power the food producing process to support the consumers and decomposers. Respiration of plants results in the consumption of CO_2 and the production of oxygen (O_2). Photosynthesis by plant life slowly enriched the atmosphere in O_2, a necessary preparatory step and ingredient to support all forms of higher animal life.

Changes in the gases of the atmosphere probably had profound effects on the surface temperature of the earth. The increase in O_2 was accompanied by a parallel decrease in the amount of CO_2 in the atmosphere because of photosynthesis. When visible rays of the sun hit the earth, they lose energy and re-radiate or reflect as invisible rays of heat (infrared radiation). Carbon dioxide, which is completely transparent to the visible light waves, does not permit the passage of the infrared rays and so holds the heat on the earth's surface. The thinning of the CO_2 blanket undoubtedly led to a temperature decrease, which perhaps was requisite for the less heat-tolerant consumers.

Preparation of the Earth's Crust for Life

According to current scientific theories, the young earth was very hot. The more dense materials such as iron, and to a lesser extent cobalt and nickel, collected to the center forming a dense molten core whose diameter is about half that of the earth. The lighter materials rose to the surface, and as the earth cooled a thin, wrinkled crust formed. Water vapor was one of the chief components of the primitive atmosphere. Viewed from outer space, earth at that time would have appeared much as the planet Venus does to us now, wrapped in a perpetual blanket of clouds. When the earth's surface was still hot, the rain that fell from the clouds would have sizzled and boiled up again into the atmosphere causing the dense blanket of clouds. Over time, the earth began to cool and rain would begin to accumulate in the depressions of the earth's crust. Eventually the earth's basins became shallow seas and the creation event referred to as the second period of time in verse 6 was accomplished, "and God made the firmament, and divided the waters which were under the firmament from the waters which were above the firmament." The next event recorded in the scriptures was in verse 9, "Let the water under the heaven be gathered together unto one place, and let the dry land appear." According to the current scientific theories of events on the surface of the young earth, the water began to accumulate on the surface and the enveloping cloud blanket, from which some water vapor had been removed, was changing. The atmosphere slowly began to be transparent due to the decrease in water vapor, and the sunlight started to directly reach the earth's surface for the first time. This transformation of the atmosphere was in preparation for the events of the fourth creation time. The corresponding scriptural account of this process is duly recorded in verses 14–17, "And God said, Let there be lights in the firmament . . . and let them . . . give light upon the earth."

The earth is composed of approximately one hundred different elements; oxygen and silicon are by far the most abundant, followed by aluminum and iron. A mineral is a composite of these elements and rocks are mixtures of minerals. Most of the land surface of modern earth is made up of granite, which is an igneous rock, that is, rock formed directly from molten material. Just below the granite is a layer of heavier igneous rock, basalt, which contains more iron compounds than granite. Basalt makes up the bottom of the ocean basin. Below the surface of the earth, the temperature increases rapidly, and at a depth of only thirty to forty miles it may be as high as 1,500°C, which is the melting point of basalt. The continents, then, are masses of granite floating on molten basalt, like great icebergs on the ocean.

In terms of the geologic time scale, the surface of the continents undergoes constant change. Contractions and shiftiness of the surface crumple the surface. The crust rises and sinks because of the motion of semi-molten material underneath. Earthquakes shake its surface, cracks form, and molten lava forces its way toward the surface under pressure from the hot interior. As a consequence of this mixture of forces, the earth's surface is not at all uniform but varies widely from place to place in its composition and its content of minerals. These variations, combined with differences in temperature, sunlight, and available water, have profound consequences on the ability to support plant life. The surface of the earth needed considerable preparation before plant life could take hold. Rocks were broken down by weathering processes, such as freezing and thawing or heating and cooling, which cause the substances in the rocks to expand and contract, thus splitting the rocks apart. Water and wind exert a scouring action that breaks the fragmented rock into smaller particles, often carrying the fragments great distances. Water enters between the particles, and soluble materials such as rock salt dissolve in the water. Water in combination with CO_2 from the air forms a mild acid that dissolves substances that will not dissolve in the water alone. Soil is that portion of the earth's crust that supports the growth and provides nutrients for higher plant forms. Modern soil is a complex mosaic composed chiefly of organic material (remains of once living organisms) and fragments of weathered rocks, some of which are changed into entirely new minerals by the action of the weathering. Ancient soil, before the invasion of plants, would have been missing the organic component. However, much weathering and breaking down of the original rock into fine particles was necessary to prepare an elementary soil for the advent of plants. Bacteria and the primitive plants such as algae were the first to gain a foothold onto the land, followed by small plants. Finally, the larger plants moved in, anchoring the soil in place with their root systems. Over time the organic composition of soil increased to the current status. This metamorphosis of the earth's rocky crust to soil if caused by natural forces that we know of, such as water, wind, and sun, would require millions to billions of years to transpire. The description by Abraham, "Let us prepare the earth to bring forth . . . plants" is perfectly consistent with the scenario just described as deduced from modern science.

The remarkable similarities between modern scientific theory and the scriptural description of the creation are astounding. There is no doubt that the text of the creation story by Moses and Abraham is of ancient origin and in the absence of God's enlightenment they could not have described the creation events that match so well with that learned by modern scientific investigation. Surely, the creation account in the scriptures is of divine origin and authored by the very Creator Himself.

Movement of Plant Life from the Oceans to Land

All available evidence strongly shows that the first plant life to appear lived in the oceans and were simple single-celled autotrophs that resembled today's forms of the blue-green algae and the green photosynthetic bacteria. Over time, the Protista or diatoms, the major component of phytoplankton, appeared and later the more complex forms of plant life arose. These life forms were still confined to a total water environment. For plant life to invade the land, considerable changes and adaptations were necessary. Again, the reference by Abraham in verse 11, "Let us prepare the earth to bring forth grass," was particularly apropos of the preparations necessary for this adaptation and invasion to take place. According to current scientific theory, plants first appeared on land about five hundred million years ago. No living thing, whether plant or animal, has yet succeeded in carrying on its life processes independent of a liquid medium. Although many organisms exist in areas far from open bodies of water, they all provide an internal liquid environment for the individual cells. Without this, the normal exchange of materials necessary for cellular metabolism could not occur. The fossil record indicates that the first land organisms lived in very moist areas, such as the shore regions of lakes and oceans. The invasion of land brought with it some very real challenges. Foremost was the danger of drying out. In the water, single-celled algae and bacteria were surrounded by a medium that brought all their nutrients to them and carried away all their metabolic wastes. At the same time, water provides a medium for osmotic exchange (the life-critical movement of liquid through semipermeable membranes). Living out of the water also made the distribution of gametes during sexual reproduction more difficult. For aquatic organisms, gamete distribution is relatively simple. More advanced terrestrial plants have developed very elaborate and sophisticated mechanisms for distributing their reproductive cells. One of the most dramatic innovations by land plants was the development of the seed. The scriptural accounts of the creation refer to this as, "Let the earth bring forth . . . the herb yielding seed." The seed allows the young plant embryo to remain dormant and protected until favorable conditions for germination occur, thus enabling the process of propagation to survive through periods of drought or frigid temperatures. Another problem land plants faced was that of cell specialization and differentiation. Simple aquatic plants were able to absorb all of their raw materials for cellular metabolism directly from their surrounding medium. Each cell was capable of taking care of its own individual needs. On land, however, support, absorption, anchorage, and storage of carbohydrate products were all special problems requiring special solutions. Differentiation of cells to perform specialized tasks produced the types of tissues that we now associate with higher plants. Xylem and phloem (the vascular system of plants), protective tissues, and meristematic tissue (primary growth-initiating cells) all serve special functions. Angiosperms, since they possess all of these types of cells in their most highly differentiated form, are considered the most advanced land plants on earth. The long and challenging process by which plants invaded the land was simply summarized by Abraham with the phrase, "Let us prepare the earth."

We must realize the events of the time periods did not necessarily finish before the events of the next period were initiated. For example, the events of the creation period three must have spanned a very long period of time, from the formation of the oceans and land to all plants including the fruit tree. According to all existing evidence, advanced plant life such as fruit trees appeared much later than some of the early events of the next creation period, such as penetration of light to the earth's surface and formation of the primitive aquatic animals (see chapter 6 for details). There is no compelling reason to assume that latter events of creation period three were complete before some of the early events of creation period four were started. Certain advantages and efficiencies could be achieved by allowing some overlap between the creation periods. By way of a modern analogy, all contemporary building projects are divided into phases of construction. A common strategy by project engineers is to overlap construction phases to achieve efficiency of time. Certainly the Gods may have used similar tactics for effectiveness.

In the manner described by the scriptural account and that deduced from science, the introduction of primitive to moderately complex plants needed to precede animal life and was necessary to prepare the earth for the diversity of life. Green plants are the principal organisms that capture the energy of the sun and make it available to other living organisms. Moreover, plants take carbon dioxide and inorganic forms of nitrogen and build complex molecules such as sugars, amino acids, and other compounds essential for the structure and function of living things. Carbon, nitrogen, and other essential elements enter the living world through the activities of these autotrophic organisms. The emphasis by Abraham on the need to prepare the earth to bring forth life is most discerning. The scholars at the time of Abraham and even Joseph Smith were not sufficiently aware of these paleoecological relationships to have deduced on their own that plant life needed to precede animal life and was necessary to prepare the earth for the diversity of life.

Genesis	**Moses**	**Abraham**
12. And the earth brought forth grass, and herb yielding seed after his kind, and the tree yielding fruit, whose seed was in itself, after his kind: and God saw it was good.	12. And the earth brought forth grass, every herb yielding seed after his kind, and the tree yielding fruit, whose seed should be in itself, after his kind; and I, God, saw that all things which I had made were good;	12. And the Gods organized the earth to bring forth grass from its own seed, and the herb to bring forth herb from its own seed, yielding seed after his kind; and the earth to bring forth the tree from its own seed, yielding fruit,

		whose seed could only bring forth the same in itself, after his kind; and the Gods saw that they were obeyed.
13. And the eveing and the morning were the third day.	13. And the evening and the morning were the third day.	13. And it came to pass that they numbered the days; from the evening until the morning they called night; and it came to pass, from the morning until the evening they called day; and it was the third time.

Much of that previously emphasized by the Abraham account is repeated in verses 12–13. The term "organized" was used again in verse 12 and reaffirms the principle of combining the eternal elements to create new life forms. The repeated use of "the third time" referring to the third creation day is found in verse 13 and stresses the variable and extended nature of this time period.

Chapter Four

Comparison of Scriptural Truths: Days 4 and 5

The essence of creation days four and five was the direct penetration of sunlight to earth's surface for the first time and the diverse formation of aquatic animal life and fowl of the air. Despite the previous co-creation of the sun and moon, their direct observation from the vantage point of the earth's surface did not take place until the fourth creation period. Modern science has come to show that this was due to the thick non-transparent nature of the early atmosphere. The writers of all three scriptural accounts could not have been aware of the delayed appearance of sunlight without the direct inspiration from the Creator himself.

Abraham brings further insight into the creation process and sequence of events by emphasizing the following pattern used by the Gods: ordered → watched → obeyed.

Abraham also indicates the laying out of a careful plan for the creation. This type of narrative strongly implies a sequential process with a waiting period in the middle while events transpired. This passage of time, perhaps extended, while the Gods watched, is very consistent with the known ancient age of the earth. Similar to the previous creation of plant life, Abraham reminds us that considerable preparation was necessary for the waters to bring forth animal life. Numerous life-sustaining cycles needed to be implemented to have a robust environment for abundant animal life. The carbon, nitrogen, and water cycles are examples of the preparation referred to by Abraham to ensure a replenishing source of nutrients.

Genesis	**Moses**	**Abraham**
14. And God said, Let there be lights in the firmament of the heaven to divide the day from the night; and let them be for signs, and for seasons, and for days, and years:	14. And I, God, said: Let there be lights in the firmament of the heaven, to divide the day from the night, and let them be for signs, and for seasons, and for days, and for years.	14. And the Gods organized the lights in the expanse of the heaven, and caused them to divide the day from the night; and organized them to be for signs and for seasons, and for days and for years.

15. And let them be for lights in the firmament of the heaven to give light upon the earth: and it was so.	15. And let them be for lights in the firmament of the heaven to give light upon the earth; and it was so.	15. And organized them to be for lights in the expanse of the heaven to give light upon the earth; and it was so.

The events of the earlier creation periods described the massive condensation of water vapor from the atmosphere to the oceans on the earth's surface. This resulted in a drastic change of the atmosphere that made it more transparent to sunlight. As the enveloping cloud blanket began to tear apart, due to the removal of water vapor, direct sunlight reached the earth's surface for the first time. The corresponding scriptural account of this process is duly recorded in verses 14–15, "And God said, Let there be lights in the firmament . . . and let them . . . give light upon the earth."

An apparent discrepancy between the scriptural account of the creation and scientific theory arises at this point, but upon closer examination mutual consistency may be realized. Current scientific evidence suggests that the entire solar system, including the sun, was formed at about the same time. Then why does the scriptural account refer to two events associated with the appearance of light? The first time, on day or time period one, is in verse 3, "and God said, Let there be light: and there was light." The second mention of lights is on day or time period four, in verses 14–16, "And God said, Let there be lights in the firmament . . . to give light upon the earth . . . and God made two great lights; the greater light to rule the day, and the lesser light to rule the night; he made the stars also."

At first glance, the appearance of light on two occasions may seem confusing, but becomes clear upon a realization that the point of reference changed between the two appearances of light. The first mention of light refers to the original creation of the solar system, including the sun, from the perspective of the Gods, whereas the second mention of light was from the surface of the earth. According to scientific evidence, the surface of the earth was dark after the original creation period due to the high density of small solid particle debris floating in the atmosphere. Eventually the atmospheric debris settled and the dull light from the sun distinguished day from night. At this stage the sun was not directly visible from earth's surface due to the gas composition of the atmosphere which absorbed the majority of light. After much time the atmosphere slowly changed composition and became transparent. The light from the previously created sun, moon, and stars became visible for the first time from the earth's surface, which was recorded as the second appearance of light (see chapter 6 for more details concerning the changes of the early atmosphere). With this further understanding, we are reminded once again of the deep and meaningful significance of the scriptural version of the creation and its astounding consistency with modern science.

Genesis	**Moses**	**Abraham**
16. And God made two great lights; the greater light to rule the day, and the lesser light to rule the night: he made the stars also.	16. And I, God, made two great lights; the greater light to rule the day, and the lesser light to rule the night, and the greater light was the sun, and the lesser light was the moon; and the stars also were made even according to my word.	16. And the gods organized the two great lights, the greater light to rule the day, and the lesser light to rule the night; with the lesser light they set the stars also.
17. And God set them in the firmament of the heaven to give light	17. And I, God, set them in the firmament of the heaven to give	17. And the Gods set them in the expanse of the heavens, to give light

upon the earth.	light upon the earth,	upon the earth,and to rule over the day and over the night, and to cause to divide the light from the darkness.
18. And to rule over the day and over the night, and to divide the light from the darkness: and God saw that it [illegible]	18. And the sun to rule over the day, and the moon to rule over the night, and to divide the light from the darkness; and I, God, saw that all things which I had made were good;	18. And the Gods watched those things which they had ordered until they obeyed.

Abraham, in verse 18, provides additional insight into the creation process, "And the gods watched those things which they had ordered until they obeyed." The sequence of events and the specific verbs used were, ordered, watched, obeyed. This detailed narrative strongly implies a sequential process with a waiting period in the middle while events transpired. This passage of time, perhaps extended, while the Gods watched, is very consistent with the known ancient age of the earth. The visual image of the Gods "snapping their fingers" and complex life forms instantly developing or appearing is contrary to the description of Abraham and to the facts of science.

Genesis	Moses	Abraham
19. And the evening and the morning were the fourth day.	19. And the evening and the morning were the fourth day.	19. And it came to pass that it was from evening until morning that it was night; and it came to pass that it was from morning until evening that it was day; and it was the fourth time.
20. And God said, Let the waters bring forth abundantly the moving creature that hath life, and fowl that may fly above the earth in the open firmament of heaven.	20. And I, God, said: Let the waters bring forth abundantly the moving creature that hath life, and fowl which may fly above the earth in the open firmament of heaven.	20. And the Gods said: Let us prepare the waters to bring forth abundantly the moving creatures that have life; and the fowl, that they may fly above the earth in the open expanse of heaven.
21. And God created great	21. And I, God, created	21. And the Gods prepared

whales, and every living creature that moveth, which the waters brought forth abundantly, after their kind, and every winged fowl after his kind: and God saw that it was good.

great whales, and every living creature that moveth, which the waters brought forth abundantly, after their kind; and I, God, saw that all things which I had created were good.

the waters that they might bring forth great whales, and every living creature that moveth, which the waters were to bring forth abundantly after their kind; and every winged fowl after their kind. And the Gods saw that they would be obeyed, and that their plan was good.

Over a million species of animals have been identified and the list grows longer the closer we look. God did not create all these species at the same time. The scriptural description provides an order and sequence to the appearance of these diverse species. Starting with verse 20 and proceeding onward the first animal life appeared in the sea as simple moving creatures; then fish of all kinds; followed by fowl; then terrestrial creatures including the mammals; and lastly humans. This diversity of animal species appeared over the span of two creation periods. Scientific dating of animal fossils establish the beginning of the simple sea-bound creatures approximately six hundred million years ago. The step-by-step creation of animal life contained in the scriptures is wholly consistent with that known from scientific findings.

Much of the insight concerning the creation of plant life provided by the three scriptural versions is likewise repeated for animal life. Verses 20 and 21 of Abraham emphasize that the Gods "prepared the waters" for the bringing forth of animal life. Verse 21 particularly implies a most interesting scenario, "the Gods prepared the waters that they might bring forth great whales." The pronoun "they" most directly refers to the noun "waters," thus implying that, as a result of the Gods' preparation, the waters sprang forth life spontaneously. Looking back from a modern day scientific perspective this scenario could easily be misinterpreted in a godless fashion. However, Abraham specifically reminds us that the Gods prepared the waters.

Just as much preparation was necessary to support plant life, considerable preparation was needed before animal life could be established. As described earlier, all life can be categorized into three groups, producers, consumers, and decomposers. Plants are the ultimate producer organisms because they harness the energy from the sun to provide power to the consumers. Animals are the principal consumer organisms on earth. Animals are consumers because they feed directly on other organisms. Some animals (herbivores) feed directly on the producers while other animals (carnivores) feed directly on other animals. The herbivores and carnivores could not exist until the producers were well established. In this interdependent manner, earth was prepared as described by Abraham for the creation of the animal kingdom.

The decomposers are both plants and animals. Familiar decomposers are the fungi and bacteria. These organisms break down the complex molecules that the producers and consumers synthesized and return them back to the environment in more elementary forms. At the same time, the decomposers are gaining their own nourishment. With the creation of the producers, consumers, and decomposers, the Gods established a perfect plan, or cyclic process, for the sustaining of life that would be self-supporting, resilient, and sustaining.

In the last part of verse 21, Abraham declares that the Gods saw that their "plan was good." The Abraham account adds the new emphasis of "plan" to the creation events. The creation was well planned and executed. This was not a trial and error experiment. After all, The Firstborn of Elohim had created millions of worlds like ours. As with any plan, time is required. The terms "plan" and "prepare" go hand-in-hand and are repeatedly part of the creation description by Abraham.

This plan referred to by Abraham included the robust recirculation of energy and matter by the producers, consumers, and decomposers. To sustain life for the population of all of God's spirit children, the earth needed a constant input of energy. The sun provides this energy and was created about six billion years ago and is estimated to be able to produce a constant source of energy for another six billion years. This should be sufficient time for all of us to work out our exaltation. As we have seen, the sun's energy is captured in the food-making processes of green plants. The energy is released again in the metabolism of both plants and animals. The matter (i.e., the atoms and molecules) that constitutes the earth and its living organisms does not have to be continually replenished from the outside. The elements are constantly recirculated through well-planned life cycles. To appreciate the intricate plan and interdependent nature of all living organisms, a brief survey of various life cycles is appropriate.

The Carbon Cycle

Nearly every compound involved in the metabolic activity of living things contains the element carbon and is termed "organic."

The self-perpetuation of the earth requires that the carbon trapped within organisms be ultimately returned to the environment in a process known as the carbon cycle. Considering the atmosphere first, the level of carbon dioxide (CO_2) is maintained by animals and plants. Animals respire and take in O_2 and release CO_2 while plants do the opposite taking in CO_2 and releasing O_2. This yin-yang relationship is part of the well-prepared plan by the Creator and maintains a constant replenishing level of CO_2 and O_2 in the atmosphere to support life.

Another route for carbon is that both plants and animals convert carbon into more complex molecules needed to sustain life, such as, carbohydrates proteins, lipids (fats), nucleic acids, vitamins, and etc. Sometimes the dead remains of plants and animals are deposited at the bottom of lakes, oceans, and under soil. By being covered by mud and water these organic materials undergo decay and get subjected to great pressure. Over long periods of time and intense pressure these organic materials change form and are converted to coal and petroleum. These forms of carbon contain high-energy bonds that were the result of the synthetic reactions of ancient plants and animals. Coal and petroleum are excellent sources of energy and are the principal sources of fuel that support the existence of modern humans.

God's offspring number in the billions, each of which needs to come upon the earth and receive bodies and work out their exaltation. The earth was carefully prepared by the Gods to contain vast sources of fuel in order to make the human population possible. To do so, enormous quantities of plants and animals had to precede humans. This preparation process referred to repeatedly by Abraham required billions of years to convert the earth to a planet that would sustain the myriad numbers of God's children.

Eventually these complex organic forms are burned and returned to the atmosphere as CO_2. Over the course of time, a single atom of carbon may have existed in a variety of compounds in a variety of different organisms. Realization of the carbon cycle enhances our appreciation of the many scriptural references of dust, such as in Moses 4:25—"for out of it wast thou taken: for dust thou wast, and unto dust shalt thou return."

The Nitrogen Cycle

Nitrogen is no less important for life than carbon. The nitrogen cycle cycle involves a number of organisms and a variety of pathways. There is no single nitrogen cycle, but a group of cycles that all interact with each other. These interdependent cycles ensure that no atoms of nitrogen are permanently withdrawn from circulation. In the atmosphere, molecular nitrogen composes 78 percent of the air. Neither green plants nor animals use this form of atmospheric nitrogen directly. Atmospheric nitrogen is converted by nitrogen-fixing bacteria to a usable form, known as nitrates, that is absorbed by leguminous plants (i.e., plants that bear their seeds in pods, such as beans or peas). Nitrates are then converted by plants into amino acids and proteins. The nitrogen in plant proteins is an essential source of nitrogen for the herbivores and, in turn, for the carnivores of the animal kingdom. These life-sustaining converted forms of nitrogen are returned to molecular nitrogen in the atmosphere by two different routes. If animals ingest the plant, protein is broken down and ultimately excreted as waste and converted back to atmospheric nitrogen by denitrifying bacteria. If, on the other hand, the plant dies, the proteins may be acted on by putrefying and denitrifying bacteria. This process converts the plant protein back to atmospheric nitrogen. These nitrogen molecules are constantly being synthesized and degraded, resulting in the cycling of nitrogen from the environment to the organism and back to the environment. In this manner, a constant source of essential nitrogen is available for life.

The Water Cycle

The last cycle that we will consider is the water cycle. The existence of living organisms depends on relatively large and continuous supplies of water. Most of the water on earth is located in the oceans. This water is constantly evaporated by the heat of the sun, and passes as vapor into the atmosphere. In the atmosphere, water condenses into clouds and eventually returns to the surface of the earth as rain or snow. Ultimately, the rain or snow runs into rivers and finds its way to the oceans. This process constitutes the water cycle. Plants and animals temporarily interrupt this cycle. Water soaking into the ground after a rain is absorbed by the roots of plants and passes into the stem and up to the leaves. Here the water is used in photosynthesis and eventually returned to the atmosphere at the leaf surface through transpiration. Animals drink water and are predominantly composed of water. This water is liberated back to the atmosphere through excretion and respiration.

The physical properties of water, which sustain it as the ubiquitous solvent of life, are unique. Water can exist in three physical states: liquid, gas (vapor), or solid (ice). The uniqueness of water is that the conversion between these physical states occurs within the temperature range commonly found on earth and that is tolerable by living organisms. At any given spot on the earth, water may exist in all three forms simultaneously. This precise temperature dependence of the physical states of water allows for an efficient water cycle.

The temperature conversion between liquid water and vapor water allows for evaporation from the earth's surface and condensation in the atmosphere. The thermodynamics of evaporation at the surface of living organisms is essential for cooling down the heat produced from metabolism, particularly in warm climates. A most unusual property of solid/ liquid water permits the existence of life in the cooler climates of earth. Water is the only compound known in which the solid (ice) state is less dense than the liquid. In other words, as water freezes it expands. Without this unique property of water, the earth would likely become a solid block of permanent ice. For example, as water cools to the freezing point in the bottom of oceans, lakes, and seas it expands and floats to the surface where it is warmed by the sun. This provides for the transfer of colder water from the bottom to warmer waters at the surface and vice versa. If this were not so, the water at the bottom of the oceans would freeze and remain as a solid block at the bottom never to thaw. As time passed, this block of ice would grow until it consumed all the liquid.

Current earth temperatures would never be sufficient to ever thaw this block of ice.

The cycles we have discussed are by no means the only ones that may be traced in nature. However, these serve to emphasize the intricate relationships that exist between the earth and living organisms. These relationships were carefully planned and are referred to by the Gods in the latter part of verse 21 in Abraham, "that their plan was good."

Genesis	**Moses**	**Abraham**
22. And God blessed them, saying, Be fruitful, and multiply, and fill the waters in the seas, and let fowl multiply in the earth.	22. And I, God, blessed them, saying: Be fruitful, and multiply, and fill the waters in the sea; and let fowl multiply in the earth;	22. And the Gods said: We will bless them, and cause them to be fruitful and multiply, and fill the waters in the seas or great waters; and cause the fowl to multiply in the earth.
23. And the evening and the morning were the fifth day.	23. And the evening and the morning were the fifth day.	23. And it came to pass that it was from evening until morning that they called night; and it came to

pass that it
was from
morning until
evening that
they called
day; and it was
the fifth time.

Again, Abraham emphasizes this creation period as the "fifth time." This provides further credence to the concept that these creation periods were not twenty-four-hour days.

Chapter Five

Comparison of Scriptural Truths: Days 6 and 7

Day six describes the creation of land animals and finally the ultimate creation of humankind. On day seven the Gods rest from their creation efforts. Referring to the creation of the land animals, Abraham specifies that the animals obeyed the plan. Perhaps this terminology indicates that the creation process was obedient or compliant with the natural laws and principles. God is the greatest scientist of all and his crowning achievement of the creation was accomplished through perfect knowledge of all natural laws and principles of science. Concerning the process of creation, Abraham provides additional insight. The concept of councils and their decision making is described. Such deliberation conjures an image of the creation process that was slow, step-by-step, and with multiple decision points along the way. To accomplish the work of the creation, the Gods came down to earth to perform specific functions, indicating the creation was very much a hands-on type of process. Abraham repeatedly provides the image of a creation that extended over long periods of time that is very consistent with the known ancient age of the earth.

Abraham provides an explanation for human sexuality. The Gods, "caused them to be fruitful and multiply." We learn from other revealed scriptures that man is commanded to cleave to their spouse and none other. These two dichotomous commandments were established as testing grounds for humans to earn the privilege of eternal increase. After the creation of humankind the Gods ended their work pertaining to the creation. Every creation period was divided into a morning and evening portion. For each of the first six creation periods the specific mention of an evening is made but not for the seventh. The distinct absence of an evening may indicate that this period is continuing even into our day. Two creations were described, a temporal and spiritual. Almost all of the scriptural description of the creation is of the temporal and only one and a half verses are devoted to the spiritual. The book of Moses provides the most insight into the spiritual creation and tells us that all things were created previously in heaven before they were temporally created on earth.

Genesis	Moses	Abraham
24. And God said, Let the earth bring forth the living creature after his kind, cattle, and creeping thing, and beast of the earth after his kind: and it was so.	24. And I, God, said: Let the earth bring forth the living creature after his kind, cattle, and creeping things, and beasts of the earth after their kind, and it was so;	24. And the Gods prepared the earth to bring forth the living creature after his kind, cattle and creeping things, and beasts of the earth after their kind; and it was so, as they had said.
25. And God made the beast of the earth after his kind, and cattle after their kind, and every thing that creepeth upon the earth after his kind: and God saw that it was good.	25. And I, God, made the beasts of the earth after their kind, and cattle after their kind, and everything which creepeth upon the earth after his kind; and I, God, saw that all these things were good.	25. And the Gods organized the earth to bring forth the beasts after their kind, and cattle after their kind, and every thing that creepeth upon the earth after its kind; and the Gods saw they would obey.

The Abraham version continues to emphasize the concept that the Gods "prepared" and "organized" the earth to bring forth animal life. This is consistent with the previous comments concerning the intricate relationships of living organisms with the earth and vice versa. These verbs used by Abraham also lend support to the time element necessarily associated with these creation periods. The latter part of verse 25 in Abraham indicates that the animals obeyed the plan. The term "obey" connotes compliance. What were the animals compliant to? Perhaps this terminology used by Abraham implies that the creation process was compliant with the natural laws and principles.

For example, Abraham may have been trying to inform us that the creation process was not accomplished by magic but through the knowledgeable exercise of eternal laws and principles of physics and chemistry. Many of these laws and principles have been discovered by modern science, but some may remain unknown. We are continually amazed by the feats of modern science, such as the take off of a jumbo 747 airplane, the wireless communication between individuals from distant parts of the planet, the laser surgery of the eye to correct poor vision, and the cloning of a sheep. As amazing as these accomplishments are, how much greater are God's accomplishments of the creation. He is the greatest scientist of all, he is omniscient and omnipotent.

These God-like attributes are achieved through perfect knowledge of all natural laws and principles of science. Of course, a perfect discipline and judgement to know when to exercise these principles must accompany this knowledge.

Genesis	Moses	Abraham
26. and God said, Let us make man in our image, after our likeness: and let them have dominion over the fish of the sea, and over the fowl of the air, and over the cattle, and over all the earth, and over every creeping thing that creepeth upon the earth.	26. And I, God, said unto mine Only Begotten, which was with me from the beginning: Let us make man in our image, after our likeness; and it was so. and I, God said: Let them have dominion over the fishes of the sea, and over the fowl of the air, and over the cattle, and over all the earth, and over every creeping thing that creepeth upon the earth.	26. And the Gods took counsel among themselves and said: Let us go down and form man in our image, after our likeness; and we will give them dominion over the fish of the sea, and over the fowl of the air, and over the cattle, and over all the earth, and over every creeping thing that creepeth upon the earth.

Now, at the final stages of the creation, the Moses account reemphasizes the role of the Savior, the Only Begotten. The Only

Begotten was with the Father from the beginning of the creation to the end, thereby earning the descriptive title of Alpha and Omega, the First and the Last, the Beginning and the End.

For the first time in the creation account, Genesis and Moses use the terms "us" and "our," thus emphasizing the plurality of Gods. Here Abraham further elaborates and introduces the concept and process of "counsel." This infers that the Gods met together to formulate a plan of action, they deliberated and perhaps the less experienced sought out advicefrom the more experienced. The formation of man was the final, culminating, and most complicated step of the creation. Every detail needed to be carefully and meticulously planned out and executed.

Genesis	**Moses**	**Abraham**
27. So God created man in his own image, in the image of God created he him: male and female created he them.	27. And I, God, created man in mine own image, in the image of mine Only Begotten created I him; male and female created I them.	27. So the Gods went down to organize man in their own image, in the image of the Gods to form they him, male and female to form they them.

No mistakes could be tolerated, for the spirit offspring of God would inherit these physical bodies for all time forward. This was not a trial-and error-process or learn-as-you-go activity.

Abraham introduces another new insight of the creation process by the phrase, "the Gods went down to organize." Abraham emphasizes that the Gods traveled to earth to perform critical functions to bring to pass the creation of man. Their role upon arrival on the earth was to "organize" so that man could be created in their own image. To find out their exact role we will have to wait until the day referred to in 2 Nephi 27:10, the "due time of the Lord . . . [when] they reveal all things from the foundation of the world unto the end thereof." The concept that man developed spontaneously or without God's direct involvement is not consistent with the Gods' visitation to earth. Whatever process was involved required their direct presence. The means of travel from God's home to earth and the time required remains a mystery.

Genesis	**Moses**	**Abraham**
28. And God blessed them, and God said unto them, Be fruitful, and multiply, and replenish the	28. And I, God, blessed them, and said unto them: Be fruitful, and multiply, and replenish the	28. And the Gods said: We will bless them. And the Gods said: We will cause them to be fruitful

earth, and subdue it: and have dominion over the fish of the sea, and over the fowl of the air, and over every living thing that moveth upon the earth.

earth, and subdue it, and have dominion over the fish of the sea, and over the fowl of the air, and over every living thing that moveth upon the earth.

and multiply, and replenish the earth, and subdue it, and to have dominion over the fish of the sea, and over the fowl of the air, and over every living thing that moveth upon the earth.

Abraham provides an explanation for human sexuality. The Gods, "caused them to be fruitful and multiply." It has been said that the strongest human drive other than hunger is the sexual appetite. The sexual attraction between male and female is a God-given attribute with a definite eternal purpose. To understand the importance and significance of why the Gods bestowed the sexual drive upon humans we must understand our role in the eternal scheme. Doctrine and Covenants 132:19–20 succinctly and powerfully reveals our potential, "Ye shall come forth in the first resurrection . . . and shall inherit thrones, kingdoms, principalities, and powers, dominions, all heights, and depths . . . which glory shall be a fulness and a continuation of the seeds forever and ever. Then shall they be gods, because they have no end; therefore shall they be from everlasting to everlasting, because they continue; then shall they be above all, because all things are subject unto them. Then shall they be gods."

The essence of our potential will be the privilege to continue our seed or to procreate into the eternities. Will this God-like privilege be granted to all? No, verse 19 tells us that only those that "abide in my covenant" will receive such. The covenant is explained in verse 19, "if a man marry a wife by my word, which is my law, and by the new and everlasting covenant, and it is sealed unto them by the Holy Spirit of promise, by him who is anointed, unto whom I have appointed this power and the keys of this priesthood." The covenant is: marriage sealed for time and eternity in the house of the Lord (temples). Furthermore, we must abide, or be true and faithful to this covenant. The scriptures are plain in describing what abide means: "Thou shalt love thy wife with all thy heart, and shalt cleave unto her and none else" (D&C 42:22).

God has blessed humankind with the desire to procreate, to be fruitful and multiply, but at the same time has commanded us to cleave only to our spouse and none other. To understand these boundaries and their significance, we must look into the specific conditions of our pre-earth state. Our spirit bodies had their beginning in the pre-earth life when we were born as the spirit children of God our Father. These spirit bodies had all the parts of mortal bodies. The brother of Jared saw Christ's spirit finger and then his whole spirit body-"I am Jesus Christ . . . this body, which ye now behold, is the body of my spirit; . . . and even as I appear unto thee to be in the spirit will I appear unto my people in the flesh" (Ether 3:14–17). We, including our eldest brother Jesus, differed from God the Father in a very important aspect. God the Father was a resurrected being, a glorified and perfected man, a personage of flesh and bones (D&C 130:22). Even though spirits have the image of our mortal bodies they apparently lacked in one very important aspect: they could not procreate offspring, neither spirit nor mortal children. To our knowledge, a spirit is not capable of procreation, this is only reserved for resurrected beings. A resurrected being is capable of producing spirit and mortal off-spring as evidenced by God being the father of our spirits as well as the literal father of Jesus' mortal body (Mosiah 15:2–3).

In our eternal quest to become like our Father, we desired this God-like capability. Two criteria were required: (1) we must keep our first estate (pre-earth life) and be added upon and receive a body and subsequent resurrection. (2) We must prove ourselves in our second estate (earth life), in particular to live within boundaries of our sexual appetites and cleave only to our spouse. Even in the eternities, procreation must be limited within the boundaries of eternal marriage. Infidelity in the eternities by resurrected beings cannot be tolerated. Eternal spirit children must be born within the bonds of eternal marriage.

For this reason, only those who have demonstrated self-control with respect to morality during earth life will be permitted such powers in the eternities. The Gods established this earth-life test by causing a strong sexual appetite for procreation yet commanding us to cleave only to our spouse. In this manner, the phrase used by Abraham, "We will cause them to be fruitful and multiply," takes on great significance.

Genesis	**Moses**	**Abraham**
29. And God said, Behold, I have given you every herb bearing seed, which is upon the face of all the earth, and every tree, in the which is the fruit of a tree yielding seed; to you it shall be for meat.	29. And I, god, said unto man: Behold, I have given you every herb bearing seed, which is upon the face of all the earth, and and every tree in the which shall be the fruit of a tree yielding seed; to you it shall be for meat.	29. And the Gods said: Behold, we will give them every herb bearing seed that shall come upon the face of all the earth, and every tree which shall have fruit upon it; yea, the fruit of the tree yielding seed to them we will give it; it shall

		be for their meat.
30. And to every beast of the earth, and to every fowl of the air, and to every thing that creepeth upon the earth, wherein there is life, I have given every green herb for meat: and it was so.	30. And to every beast of the earth, and to every fowl of the air, and to everything that creepeth upon the earth, wherein I grant life, there shall be given every clean herb for meat; and it was so, even as I spake.	30.And to every beast of the earth, and to every fowl of the air, and to everything that creepeth upon the earth, behold, we will give them life, and also we will give to them every green herb for meat, and all these things shall be thus organized.
31. And God saw every thing that he had made, and, behold it was very good. And the evening and the morning were the sixth day.	31. And I God, saw everything that I had made, and, behold, all things which I had made were very good; and the evening and the morning were the sixth day.	31. And the Gods said: We will do everything that we have said, and organize them; and behold, they shall be very obedient. And it came to pass that it was from evening until morning they called night; and it came to pass that it

was from morning until evening that they called day; and they numberd the sixth time.

Abraham frequently uses the term "obedient" following the various creation periods. In verse 31, specifically referring to the creation of humans Abraham says, "they shall be very obedient." Certainly Abraham was not inferring that humans would be obedient in the traditional sense of keeping God's commandments. More likely, Abraham was referring to a different type of obedience, the adherence to the creation plan. Perhaps Abraham's comments were more pertinent to the mechanism of creation. The Gods carefully planned the creation step-by-step and utilized the natural laws and principles of the universe to accomplish their goal. As their plans unfolded, each step was obedient to their expectations, including the creation of man and our inter-relationship to all of God's other creations.

Verse 31 in Abraham further emphasizes the long duration of the creation times by the phrase "And it came to pass." This emphasizes the passage of time and infers long creation periods.

Genesis	Moses	Abraham
1. Thus the heavens and the earth were finished, and all the host of them.	1. Thus the heaven and the earth were finished, and all the host of them.	1. And thus we will finish the heavens and the earth, and all the host of them.
2. And on the seventh day God ended his work which he had made; and he rested on the seventh day from all his work which he had made.	2. And on the seventh day I, God, ended my work, and all things which I had made; and I rested on the seventh day from all my work, and all things which I had made were finished, and I, God, saw that they were good;	2. And the Gods said among themselves; On the seventh time we will end our work, which we have counseled; and we will rest on the seventh time from all our work which we have counseled.
3. And God blessed the seventh day, and sanctified it: because that in it he had rested from all his work which God created and made.	3. And I, God, blessed the seventh day, and sanctified it; because that in it I had rested from all my work which I, God, had created and made.	3. And the Gods concluded upon the seventh time, because that on the seventh time they would rest from all their works which they (the Gods)

counseled among themselves to form; and sanctified it. And thus were their decisions at the time that they counseled among themselves to form the heavens and the earth.

Again Abraham reemphasizes the concept of councils in the creation planning. He further specifies that decisions were made at the time. Apparently, choices and options regarding the creation were made, since decisions were involved. With any process, multiple ways of achieving the same endpoint are usually possible. So too with the creation, the final end product was clear, but much discussion, counseling, and decisions regarding the process were probably necessary. Such deliberation portrays an image of the creation process that was slow, step-by-step, with multiple decision points along the way. Abraham, provides a completely different image of the creation process than the six twenty-four-hour creation days envisioned by some.

Each of the creation periods is divided into a morning and evening phase. These represent divisions of time that represent the beginning and ending portions of a given creation period. Verse 31 of Abraham defines these divisions as, "from evening until morning they called night; . . . it was from morning until evening that they called day." All of the first six creation periods specifically mention a morning and evening portion of the creation period. However, the mention of a morning and evening for the seventh creation is conspicuously absent. This distinct change for the seventh day suggests that this day has not yet ended. The evening of the seventh day continues into our day. The rest associated with the seventh period specifically refers to the work of creation. In verse 3, Abraham specifies, "and the Gods concluded . . . they would rest from all their works which they (the Gods) counseled among themselves to form." However, God's ongoing other work "to bring to pass the eternal life of man" was far from over. An example of God's continued other work is found in John 5:17 when Jesus was found healing the sick on the Sabbath. "But Jesus answered them, My Father worketh hitherto, and I work." After the creation of Adam and Eve, God ceased from his work of creating new life-forms. The fossil record provides further confirmation of the end of God's creation activities. According to the fossils, many new species came into existence before the introduction of humans.

In the years of human history, the documented formation of a new species has been nil.

Genesis	**Moses**	**Abraham**
4. These are the generations of the heavens and of the earth when they were created, in the day that the Lord God made the earth and the heavens,	4. And now, behold, I say unto you, that these are the generations of the heaven and of the earth, when they were created, in the day that I, the Lord God, made the heaven and the earth,	4. And the gods came down and formed these the generations of the heavens and of the earth, when they were formed in the day that the Gods formed the earth and the heavens,

All three creation accounts provide a clear example of the multiple or flexible usage of the word *day*. Verse 4 is a general summary of the entire creation that circumscribed all of the six to seven creation periods. Here, the term "in the day" does not refer to one specific twenty-four-hour creation period but to a much longer period of time. This example for the use of day provides internal consistency for the previous interpretations signifying an extended period of time.

Genesis	**Moses**	**Abraham**
5. And every plant of the field before it	5. And every plant of the field before it	5. According to all that which they

was in the earth, and every herb of the field before it grew: for the Lord God had not caused it to rain upon the earth, and there was not a man to till the ground.	was in the earth, and every herb of the field before it grew.For I, the Lord God, created all things of which I have spoken, spiritually, before they were naturally upon the face of the earth. For I, the Lord God, had not caused it to rain upon the face of the earth. And I, the Lord God, had created all the children of men; and not yet a man to till the ground; for in heaven created I them; and there was not yet flesh upon the earth, neither in the water, neither in the air;	had said concerning every plant of the field before it was in the earth, and every herb of the field before it grew; for the Gods had not caused it to rain upon the earth. When they counseled to do them, and had not formed a man to till the ground.
6. But there went up a mist from the earth,	6. But I, the Lord God, spake, and	6. But there went up a mist from the earth,

and watered the whole face of the ground.	there went up a mist from the earth, and watered the whole face of the ground.	and watered the whole face of the ground.
7. And the Lord God formed man of the dust of the ground, and breathed into his nostrils the breath of life; and men became a living soul.	7. And I, the Lord God, formed man from the dust of the ground, and breathed into his nostrils the breath of life; and man became a living soul, the first flesh upon the earth, the first man also; nevertheless, all things were before created; but spiritually were they created and made according to my word.	7. And the Gods formed man from the dust of the ground, and took his spirit (that is, man's spirit), and put it in him; and breathed into his nostrils the breath of life, and man became a living soul.

This portion of the creation account has resulted in much unnecessary controversy. Two descriptions of the creation exists, one is contained in chapter 1 of Genesis while the other is in chapter 2 of Genesis (along with the corresponding accounts in Moses and Abraham). Some have suggested that the description in the chapter 1 of Genesis represents a spiritual creation while chapter 2 represents a temporal creation. Others have interpreted them vice versa (Skousen, 1953, 18–24; Ross, 1998, 69–70). Critics have attacked the two creation descriptions as inconsistent and incompatible. Verse 5 of the Moses account adds a very important perspective with a description of the spiritual creation, "For I, the Lord God, created all things, of which I have spoken, spiritually, before they were naturally on the face of the earth." Thus, two creations did occur, first the spiritual followed by the temporal. The description of the two creations is very different, one contains many more details than the other.

The simplest and most straightforward interpretation is the following; the only description of the spiritual creation is contained in verse 5 and the last portion of verse 7. All other descriptions refer to the temporal creation. God has given us much more information regarding the temporal creation because we currently exist in the temporal world. All of the clues left behind by fossils, etc., bare witness and testimony of the divine creation of the temporal world that we see all about us. The scriptures are replete on this point: Psalm 19:1, "The heavens declare the glory of God; and the firmament sheweth his handywork"; Psalm 85:11, "Truth shall spring out of the earth"; and Romans 1:20, "For the invisible things of him from the creation of the world are clearly seen, being understood by the things that are made, even his eternal power and Godhead; so that they are without excuse."

Chapter Six

Comparison of Sequence of Events from Scripture and Science

Evidence from multiple fields of science demonstrate the creation to have been a gradual process that proceeded as time progressed from simple organisms to more complex. Science discovered this within the last few hundred years, but scriptural accounts of the creation described such a scenario many thousands of years ago. The scriptural account contains many descriptions of creation events that have remarkable similarity to that deduced independently through modern scientific investigation. Science describes the origin of the universe by the "big bang" theory which preceded the formation of earth. Science describes the earliest known entity and the main ingredient of the big bang to be electromagnetic radiation or photons of which light is a component. Similarly, the scriptures first mention the formation of Heaven followed by the earth. Likewise, the scriptures refer to earliest mention of matter as intelligence, or light and truth, or spirit element. The scientific terms of electromagnetic radiation, photon, and anti-matter are possibly synonymous with the scriptural words of intelligences, light and truth, and spirit element. Furthermore, Joseph Smith taught that spirits were made of matter which came from intelligence or light. Thus Joseph Smith taught of the interconversion of light, matter, and energy long before Einstein derived his famous equation of $E = mc^2$.

The sequence for the introduction of life forms is totally consistent with the scientifically derived historical record. The similarity between the scriptures and science is so striking that approximate dates for the scripture-based creation periods can be assigned. The scriptures report a limited number of events and contain the briefest highlights of God's activities. The recorded events reflect what is most important for all generations to know. The brevity and simplicity enhance the emphasis on the essential theme: A loving God prepared a beautiful earth that would sustain and provide for his children while they worked out their eternal life. Only the most recent few generations would have the knowledge and sophistication to appreciate more detail. For modern man, God left an abundant amount of clues for us to piece together. For every creation event described there are clear and identifiable corresponding parallel details available from science. We will discuss a few of the more obvious parallels, but with a little imagination the reader will discover many more.

Formation of the Heavens

The universe and earth had a definite beginning according to both scripture and science. Scriptural accounts use the powerful imagery of, "In the beginning God created the heaven and earth." The first event mentioned in the scriptures was the creation of heaven. The comparable event according to science was the origin of the universe. The descriptor used by modern physicist is a creative blast or the "big bang." The big bang has been dated to about seventeen billion years ago (see chapter 9) while the earth dates back to about five billion years. Scripture and science both agree that the creation of heavens preceded the earth.

In the late 1920s Edwin Hubble (for which the famed Hubble telescope is named) made a startling discovery. He discovered the stars in the firmament are not fixed or stationary, but the universe is rapidly expanding (Hubble, 1929). This expansion is the movement of the stars away from each other. Traces of this expansion are directly observable by modern instrumentation and can be tracked back to an origin or starting point. This starting point is referred to as the big bang, or the original explosion that resulted in the formation of the universe. The big bang was in principle an enormous thermonuclear detonation of incomprehensible magnitude.

According to theory, the big bang arose from the compression of the energy of the universe into a super-dense space. The original energy of the universe was composed chiefly of electromagnetic radiation, which is a fundamental physical force that arises from the interaction of charged particles. Electromagnetic radiation travels in bits of energy known as photons and in the pattern of waves. These waves have a broad range of frequencies that include the shortest gamma rays to the longest radio waves and including visible light. At this stage, the high-energy photons of electromagnetic radiation far outnumbered the particles of matter (protons, electrons, neutrons, and antimatter). However, there was a continual interchange between the photons and the particles of matter.

Einstein's famous equation $E = mc^2$ (where E stands for energy, m for mass, and c for the speed of light) helps describe this situation in which the energy of the photons is converted into mass and vice versa. Elementary particles constitute matter and antimatter. Examples of ordinary particles of matter are the protons, electrons, and neutrons. Particles of antimatter are the opposite of ordinary particles and are called antiparticles. An antiparticle exactly resembles its corresponding ordinary particle in every property except its charge is reversed. Antiparticles are composed of positrons, antiprotons, and antineutrons. When an ordinary particle collides with its antiparticle, the two parties destroy each other releasing energy in a process referred to as annihilation.

At the critical moment of the big bang, the compression of this enormous energy of the universe reached a critical state and the explosion that started the expansion process reversed its direction. Matter was repeatedly being formed and annihilated or burned up. A slight asymmetry between matter and antimatter resulted in leaving approximately 0.1 to 1 billion photons of light for every atom of matter formed (a ratio that still remains today), and a complete loss or annihilation of antimatter.

The billions of galaxies in the observable cosmos are comprised of this unburned matter of ordinary particles. This asymmetry between matter and antimatter is not just a guess; it is a fundamental part of modern particle physics that has been verified in experiments using high-velocity accelerators to collide atoms.

The explosive nuclear fireworks of the big bang resulted in fusion reactions that built up deuterium and helium nuclei (simple atoms, deuterium contains one neutron, one proton, and one electron, while helium has two neutrons, two protons, and two electrons). The temperatures resulting from this explosion were so high that over the next three hundred thousand years whenever an electron and proton combined into a neutral hydrogen atom (simple atom with one proton and one electron), it was immediately split apart by one of the omnipresent photons. Gradually the energy of the photons dropped and they lost their potency for splitting atoms.

At that moment when the photons lost their potency, the universe became transparent. This happened because the photons no longer interacted so intensely with the atoms; the photons flew and continue to fly across space unimpeded except for a slight shift to longer wavelengths due to the expansion of the universe in a phenomenon known as the "Doppler effect." This Doppler effect is observable by modern instrumentation in every direction into space. The observed abundance of helium and deuterium (the make up of present stars has been measured and helium was found to be approximately 25 percent of their total mass) now present in stars match the predicted amounts that would be formed in this cosmic explosion. These are some of the fossil evidences of the primeval fireball of the big bang.

The scriptures provide a prodigious parallel to the big bang theory of science. Science describes the earliest known entity as electromagnetic radiation or photons of which light is a component. The scriptures describe our pre-existent spirits as intelligence, or light and truth, or spirit element. Doctrine and Covenants 93:29 speaks of the beginning, "Intelligence, or the light of truth, was not created or made, neither indeed can be." Abraham tells us intelligences "were organized before the world was." Our spirit bodies were born from spirit element. Spirits were organized from spirit element, or intelligences, or light. The prophet Joseph Smith taught that this spirit element has always existed, and it is co-eternal with God (Smith, 1972, 352–54).

Joseph Smith sounds as though he had seen a vision of the big bang, particularly the annihilation of matter and antimatter and the production of photons of light when he said, "God had materials to organize the world out of chaos-chaotic matter, which is element and in which dwells all the glory" (Smith, 1972, 351). Perhaps chaos-chaotic matter is Joseph's description for matter and antimatter out of which flow light or glory. Doctrine and Covenants 131:7–8 specifies that "There is no such thing as immaterial matter. All spirit is matter but it is more fine or pure, and can only be discerned by purer eyes. We cannot see it: but when our bodies are purified we shall see that it is all matter." Joseph Smith was teaching us about the interconversion of light, energy, and matter long before Einstein derived his famous equation. The scientific terms of electromagnetic radiation, photon, matter, and antimatter are possibly synonymous with the scriptural words of intelligences, light of truth, and spirit element.

Formation of the Earth

The scriptures describe the creation of earth in six periods of time while science divides the history of earth into four long stretches of time called eons. Eons are subdivided into eras which are divided into periods which are divided into epochs. The length of these time divisions are based on important changes in the fossil records and as a result are not of equal length.

The first creation period according to the scriptures was the formation of earth and light. Science tells us that the earth and sun were formed in a similar time frame about 4.6 billion years ago. The description by Abraham of "empty and desolate" is very consistent to what we know from science. Initially, the surface of the earth would have been very dark, despite the co-existence of the sun, due to the high density of debris and solid particles floating in the surrounding atmosphere. Over time, gravity pulled the debris from the surrounding atmosphere to the surface of the earth in a process known as accretion. As described in the scriptures, this resulted in the first penetration of light to the earth's surface sometime after the initial formation of the earth and sun. At this stage, morning and night could be distinguished, but the sun, stars, and moon were not directly visible due to the translucent nature of the gasses in the early atmosphere. The daylight may have resembled a very overcast or gloomy day. During this time the earth was empty and desolate because life was compatible with neither the atmosphere nor the harsh conditions that existed. In this fashion, the early history of the earth is very consistent with the limited description provided in the scriptures.

Creation period two in the scriptures was centered on water. Particularly the separation of the vapor water in the atmosphere from the liquid water on the surface or oceans. The scientific parallel to this period is incredible. The earliest earth was chiefly molten rock with a thin crust that grew in thickness as the earth slowly cooled down. Initially, all the water would be expected to exist as vapor due to the high temperatures on the newly formed surface. The condensation of water vapor to form liquid and the sequential evaporation at the surface served as a cooling mechanism for the massive new planet. As cooling of the earth's surface proceeded, condensed water from the atmosphere began to accumulate in depressions on the surface. Over time great oceans and seas were formed. Evidence shows that the oceans formed about two hundred million years after the initial formation of the earth. One example of such evidence was reported in 2001. An international team of scientist discovered crystals of the mineral zircon that were determined to be 4.4 billion years old. Zircon, made up of the elements zirconium, silicon, and oxygen, is a hard, long lasting mineral that resists erosion and weathering. Through chemical analysis of the zircon, they determined that liquid water probably existed on the earth's surface when the crystal was formed. They concluded that the earth's crust and oceans might have formed about two hundred million years after the planet had taken shape.

Creation period three, according to the scriptures, was concerned with the formation of dry land and the development of plant life. Geologists have evidence that large masses of continental crust had formed by 3.5 billion years ago. There is evidence that plate tectonics have been active for at least two billion years. Regarding the sequential events of the creation, the formation of dry land as described by the scriptures has the same sequential position and a time frame congruent with the geology.

Formation of Life

The sequence of events from the scriptures are vague and incomplete. However, they clearly establish the following order: beginning with plants (verse 11) → creatures from the oceans (early verse 20) → fowls (late verse 20) → land animals (verse 24) → and ultimately man (verse 27). The sequence of events determined from modern science is remarkably similar: beginning with primitive plant life → primitive sea life → fish → fowl → land animals → and ultimately man (more details, additional species, and time dependence have been determined by science, but were not included here for comparative clarity). The appearance of species is identical between scripture and science. The similarity is striking and convincing. Hebrews 2:4 says, "God also bearing them witness, both with signs and wonders," and Doctrine and Covenants 6:28 says, "and in the mouth of two or three witnesses shall every word be established." The convergence of two independent sources of truth, the scriptures and science, stands as a powerful testimony of the creation and its divine origin.

A closer look at the similarities of the scriptural account and science provides additional insight. The creation of plants described in verse 11 of Genesis, Moses, and Abraham describe the formation of vegetation in the following order: grass → herbs yielding seed → and fruit trees. Evidence from modern academic studies of paleontology and botany, which consider the complexity of fertilization and the reproductive life cycles of plants, describe the origin of plant life to have begun with the simplest one-celled photosynthetic organism and to have developed over time with the appearance of more complex plant life. Algae, moss, ferns, and horsetails or "snake grass" are examples of the most primitive plant life. The next round of plant life to appear was the gymnosperms meaning "naked seeds." These are seed-bearing plants whose seeds are not covered by a protective tissue. Examples of gymnosperms are epedra (type of shrub with scale-like leaves) and conifers (yews, junipers, firs, spruces, pines, hemlock, and cypresses). The most complex of the plant kingdom and the most recent to appear are the angiosperms meaning "seeds borne in a vessel," that is, enclosed by definite layers of tissue. Another characteristic of this class is the appearance of flowers of some kind. This is a richly diverse group including annuals, perennials, nonconiferous trees and shrubs.

Trees possessing fleshy fruit, such as the apple, fall into this class.

Referring back to the order of vegetation listed in verse 11 of the scriptures, much similarity exists to that borne out by modern science with one exception. The details of the scriptural description are generic, and meant for all ages and people of all levels of education. For example, the grasses mentioned in verse 11 were the first vegetation mentioned however, modern science has shown that the most primitive vegetation was algae, moss, ferns, and snake grass. The "true grasses" (grains, lawn, etc) have been classified by modern taxonomists in a more advanced plant class. This apparent discrepancy in the otherwise numerous compelling consistencies may be due to our incomplete knowledge. The herb yielding seed referred to in verse 11 could well describe the class of plants known as gymnosperms. The specific reference to "seed" connotes the next level of plant complexity beyond the primitive algae, moss, ferns, and snake grass. Finally, the last class of plant life mentioned in verse 11 were the fruit trees. This is the most complex and modern class of plants that today are known as angiosperms. The fruit provide a protective cover for the seed. With this realization, the coming forth of plant life as described in the scriptures is precisely that discovered by modern science.

Comparison of the time frame from scientific history and the creation events suggest the third creation period extended for a very long time. It started with the formation of dry land about 3.5 billion years ago and did not end until the fruit tree/angiosperms were created about one hundred to one hundred fifty million years ago. We must realize the events of each of the time periods did not necessarily finish before the events of the next period were initiated. For example, as shown in the next paragraph, the events of the fourth creation day or time period, the change of the atmosphere to become transparent to sunlight, occurred about three billion years ago. The events of the third day or time period required much time and were not complete until the complex angiosperms such as the fruit tree appeared. These complex plants did not appear until long after the fourth creation period started. Thus the events of the third creation time were ongoing while other creation periods were initiated.

The fourth creation period of the scriptures principally involved the maturation of the atmosphere to a transparent stage such that lights from the heavens (sun, moon, and stars) could be visually seen from the earth's surface. Again, the scientific evidence bares witness of this atmospheric transformation in a consistent time frame. For example, geological evidence shows that the atmosphere underwent major composition changes about two billion years ago. The early atmosphere was opaque to light and contained little or no oxygen. About two billion years ago certain kinds of iron ores created in oxygen-poor environments stopped forming. Instead, large deposits of red sandstone formed. The red color results from iron reacting with oxygen to form iron oxide, or common rust. The red sandstone deposits observed today are evidence that earth's atmosphere changed over time to contain oxygen.

The increase in atmospheric oxygen was a result of the plant life created in the previous time period. Over time, plant-life consumed substantial amounts of CO_2 in the primitive atmosphere and through photosynthesis expired O_2 resulting in the gradual balance of about 20 percent found in the modern atmosphere. This atmospheric transformation was preparatory to the survival of animal life. Animals require O_2 and expire CO_2, providing a stable cyclic balance of these life-supporting gases. This atmospheric change two billion years ago also resulted in a visual change. The new compositions of atmospheric gases are transparent to visible light, and for the first time the heavenly bodies became distinctly visible. These heavenly bodies were previously created about 2.5 billion years earlier along with the earth. But, due to the opaqueness of the early atmospheric gases, only dull and nondirect sunlight penetrated to the surface of the earth. Prior to the fourth creation period, day was distinguishable from night, but the direct observation of the heavenly bodies was not visible from the earth's surface.

Some Bible critics have found fault with the repeated creations of the light, darkness, day, and night on the first and fourth creation days. However, these criticisms vanish by understanding the change of atmosphere and the different point of reference between the first and fourth creation day. Through further light and knowledge, this apparent criticism is diametrically converted into a most convincing argument for the divine authorship of the scriptural-based creation.

With light, sufficient O_2 in the atmosphere, dry land, oceans, and diversity of plant life as a primary food source, earth was ready to support rapid growth of animal life. Time period five of the creation account is marked by abundant formation of animal life. An amazing parallel also marks this creation period in scientifically derived history. About five hundred million years ago the earth went through an explosion of marine animal life referred to as the Cambrian explosion. This expansion of life forms is evident from the fossil record and actually occurred over tens of millions of years. The earliest abundant fossils of this era consisted of only a few kinds of organisms and, over the course of time, the number of species greatly increased. Most fossil organisms found from this period are invertebrates (animals without a backbone), such as corals, mollusks (clams and snails), and trilobites (flat-shelled sea animals).

Birds are dated back to about two hundred million years ago and the earliest whales to about fifty million years ago. The creation of these abundant forms of marine life spanned the period of five hundred million years to fifty million years ago. All three scriptural accounts use the phrase, "waters bring forth abundantly the moving creatures," when referring to the fifth creation period. This is an excellent description that corresponds to the Cambrian explosion of marine animal life. The limited sequence of animal life described is in exact parallel order as deduced from the fossil record. The sequence of animal life from the scriptures is marine creatures → fowl → whales. The term, "moving creatures" found in the scriptures is a particularly good description of the early marine invertebrates.

Day six of the creation account specifies the formation of land mammals and ultimately humans. Again, consistency between the scriptural accounts and science may be found in this creation period. The first evidence of land mammals dates back to about one hundred fifty million years ago, and as discussed (see chapter 10) humans appeared about thirty thousand years ago. The sixth creation period spanned the years of about one hundred fifty million years through thirty thousand years ago.

The seventh creation period is marked by a time of rest from the creation efforts. The parallel from science is that the origin of new species ended near the same time as the creation of humans. According to the fossil record, new life forms proliferated through the ages prior to the introduction of humans. Once humans came on the scene the introduction of new species plummeted to near zero. Some botanists may argue for a continued speciation into modern day. However, many experts would argue that the differentiation observed in plants by field observers represent new strains rather than new species.

A testimony of the divine creation may be strengthened by the realization that the scriptural account of the creation was not a random coincidence to that independently discovered by science, but rather the symbolic communication from the Creator Himself. The scriptural recitation of the creation is meaningful and satisfactory for early man as well as the most learned modern scholar. As new scientific truths are learned the scriptural account also takes on added significance and detail.

Time Table

Below is an estimated timetable for the creation. Dates were determined by correlation of the scriptural descriptions with the scientific record. Ending dates were assumed to terminate before the next creation period started, except for periods three and seven for which specific information was available. All dates are approximations.

Creation Period	Approximate Start (years)	Approximate End (years)
1. Created earth	4.6 billion	4.4 billion
2. Divided waters from firmament	4.4 billion	3.5 billion
3. Separated dry land from waters; created plants	3.5 billion	125 million
4. Changed atmosphere; penetration of sunlight	2 billion	500 million
5. Created sea animals and fowl	500 million	150 million
6. Created land animals and humans	150 million	30,000
7. Rest	30,000	on-going

Chapter Seven

Truths from Molecular Biology

God has left many microscopic clues of how living organisms were created. Modern biochemical investigations are revealing details concerning the creation. The blueprint for all living organisms is coded within their DNA. A remarkable finding is that all forms of life use the same language for reading and storing the vital information within the DNA blueprint. This code of information is universal for all life on earth. The ubiquitous nature of the DNA code is a profound testimony of the divine nature of the creation. God used the same optimal biochemical processes for all of his creations. The cytochrome c story provides another microscopic example of the mechanism used by the Creator.

Cytochrome c is a vital enzyme that plays a similar role in most living organisms. The linear amino acid sequence of this protein has been determined for approximately one hundred different species of organisms. The sequence for these different species varies considerably and a most amazing pattern was observed. The organisms considered the most simple had the greatest differences in their amino acid sequence compared to the most advanced. An order of creation events could be deduced from the degree of differences in the sequence of their cytochrome c molecules. The time pattern for the introduction of organisms deduced from the cytochrome c comparison was completely similar to the creation order reflected from the scriptures. The evidence shows that the Gods used the same standard framework for life such as cytochrome c. As new species were created over long periods of time, the majority of the framework remained constant but a few amino acids were mutated to create the next more complex life form.

Universal Code

The ability to reproduce is a defining attribute of a living organism. A crowning achievement of the twentieth century was the deciphering of the genetic universal code. All living organisms on earth have a blueprint known as DNA (deoxyribonucleic acid) which contains all the essential information for the organism to reproduce. Upon growth and reproduction the blueprint is read or uncoded to make all the essential components for that organism. For simple organisms the amount of blueprint is smaller than for complex organisms such as humans. All of the essential details, codes, and cellular machinery to read these blueprints have been identified, isolated, and studied. The amazing revelation is that all living organisms use a common or universal code.

DNA is a linear strand of four different molecules referred to as bases that are arranged in unique sequences thousands of bases long. The complexity of life is encrypted into the sequence or linear arrangement of these DNA bases. The manner in which a cell deciphers this blueprint is to start at one end of the DNA strand and read the sequence of three contiguous DNA bases at a time. The exact order of the three DNA bases constitute the critical code referred to as a codon. The codon is the signal for one of twenty amino acids that are assembled into polymers known as proteins that contain a unique sequence that was encoded by the DNA. Proteins are the biomolecules that perform most of the vital functions to support life.

The remarkable finding is that all forms of life use the same language of codons for storing this vital information within the DNA blueprint. This code of information is universal for all life on earth. Indeed, at the molecular level the distinguishing feature between a bacterium and human is in the exact linear arrangement of codons within the DNA. Human strands of DNA can be inserted into microorganisms and the cellular machinery of the host cell will properly function to produce human proteins. The recent advance of a new industry referred to as biotechnology has spawned from this interchangeability.

The ubiquitous nature of the universal code is a profound testimony of creation by a supreme being. The same God that created the simple single-celled organisms created the most complex multicelled organisms. For all his creations, the Creator used the same optimal biochemical processes. The creation was not an experiment, with iterative attempts to find the ultimate formula for life. But instead, that which was done had been done before (i.e., "worlds without number" [Moses 1:33] had been created) and the best biochemistry was used throughout and for all of life.

Most recently, the exact sequence for the entire DNA of a human was determined. The human genome contains approximately three billion bases. The ability to accomplish this miraculous task was the culmination of countless person-years of scientific pursuit. Numerous species of mammals have been cloned and humans appear imminent. Genetic engineering to correct abnormalities is underway and becoming a reality. Such advances in technology engender many new ethical concerns. However, we must remember the purpose of our earthly life: "To bring to pass the immortality and eternal life of man" (Moses 1:39); "Then shall they be gods, because they have all power" (D&C 132:20). Modern science is unlocking the mysteries of the creation of life. We may beuncovering the very principles and laws used by God himself to originate life. We must remain in the bounds of ethicality yet embrace that which will draw us closer to our ultimate goal, to be gods.

Cytochrome c Story

God has left many microscopic clues of how living organisms were created that are being revealed through research in modern life science laboratories. A most insightful example of the mechanism for creation is provided by the cytochrome c story.

Cytochrome c is an essential enzyme involved in the transfer of electrons that are critical for the synthesis of the energy-rich molecules of ATP (adenosine triphosphate). Cytochrome c has been widely studied in the laboratory because it is relatively easy to isolate and is small for proteins, consisting of only about one hundred amino acids. All plants, animals, and aerobic (requires air) microorganisms contain cytochrome c molecules that function perfectly well.

The cytochrome c's from many and widely varied organisms (more that one hundred at last count) were purified and the amino acid sequence determined. Should we expect the same amino acid sequence of these molecules for different organisms, since they have the same functional role? The surprising finding was that the sequence varied considerable throughout the species. Approximately 75 percent of the amino acid sequence was found to vary between the different species. An even more amazing result was that organisms considered the most simple (i.e., yeasts and molds) had the greatest differences in their amino acid sequence compared to the most advanced (i.e., mammals).

Using humans as our reference point, the last of the creation events, the number of differences between the species was directly related to the order of events described in the scriptural creation accounts. For example, the greater the difference from humans in their amino acid sequences the earlier in time was an organism's creation described. The more similar their cytochrome c molecules the closer in time was their creation. An order of creation events could be deduced from the degree of differences in the sequence of the cytochrome c molecules that reflected the creation order in the scriptures.

The most different cytochrome c sequences were the simple plants such as the algae (euglena) which contain about fifty amino acid differences compared to humans and are referred to as "grass" in verse 11 of Genesis, Moses, and Abraham. Continuing with the plant kingdom, the more modern complex plants such as the gymnosperms, or "herb yielding seed," and the angiosperms, or "fruit tree," as referenced in verse 11 have fewer cytochrome c sequence differences than the simple plants. For example, a single gymnosperm known as the ginkgo has thirty-six amino acids different and ten angiosperms (wheat, mung bean, castor, sesame, sunflower, cauliflower, buckwheat, pumpkin, abutilon, and cotton) have an average of about thirty-five amino acids different than the over-lapping regions of human cytochrome c.

A sufficient number of gymnosperm and angiosperm cytochrome c's have not been reported to establish a consistent difference between them. Thus far, the order of plant life mentioned in verse 11 of the creation accounts has the same order as that obtained from the extent of diversity of the amino acid sequence of their cytochrome c molecules.

A similar observation exists for the animal kingdom. The scriptures indicate that the plants were created prior to the "moving creatures" from the water. Fish such as tuna, carp, and dogfish have a range of seventeen to twenty-three amino acid differences (as compared to humans). Indeed, compared to humans, the plants have more differences in their cytochrome c sequences than fish. Continuing on with the animal kingdom, the scriptural accounts describe the appearance of fowl followed by land animals and ultimately humans. The cytochrome c's from fowl such as penguin, chicken, turkey, pigeon, and duck have a range of eleven to thirteen amino acid differences whereas the land animals such as kangaroo, rabbit, dog, horse, pig, cattle, sheep, and monkey have a range of ten to one amino acid differences, respectively. Based on this criteria—amino acid differences from humans—fowl preceded land animals which preceded humans.

As described in the cytochrome c story, modern biochemical investigations are revealing details concerning the creation. The evidence indicates that the Gods used a standard framework for life, such as the enzyme cytochrome c. As new species were created over long periods of time, the majority of the framework remained constant but a few amino acids were mutated to create the next more complex life form. This provides considerable insight into the mechanism of creation but does not provide any clues as to how this mutation process occurred.

God tells us in Doctrine and Covenants 93:53, "hasten to . . . obtain a knowledge . . . of laws of God and man, and all this for the salvation of Zion." Modern science is revealing the mysteries of the creation. Doctrine and Covenants 6:7 says to "seek . . . for wisdom, and behold, the mysteries of God shall be unfolded unto you." Nephi further confirms this concept in 1 Nephi 10:19, "For he that diligently seeketh, shall find; and the mysteries of God shall be unfolded unto them, by the power of the Holy Ghost, as well in these times as in times of old . . . and in times to come." We live in a marvelous time of the earth, one in which the mysteries of God are being unfolded, and we should adhere to Nephi's admonition in 2 Nephi, 9:40, "the righteous . . . love the truth." The Lord has revealed much, but all truth has not been revealed. He expects us to use our intellect and logic to deduce as much truth as possible. Through modern scientific investigation we are appreciating the deep significance of the creation story that has been revealed through the scriptures. Only the Creator Himself, could have written a description thousands of years ago that stands the test of modern science.

Chapter Eight

Reckoning of Time

Scriptures revealed through the Prophet Joseph Smith, particularly the Book of Abraham, shed immense light on the reckoning of time and its relationship to the creation. A great star named Kolob is nearest the throne of God and has the same time reckoning of God. One day in God's time reckoning represents one thousand years on earth. Abraham further instructs that these differences in time reckoning are due to different rates of planetary revolution. This revelation was most revolutionary, since the spherical nature of the earth and the relationship between time and rotation were not understood during Abraham's era.

Abraham describes that, prior to the fall of Adam, time was reckoned according to God's time reckoning, suggesting the rotation rate of the ancient earth may be quite different than the rotation rate in modern times. Evidence for dramatic changes in the earth's rotation rate during ancient history is verified by scientific data. This change in rotation rate may have been caused by the much closer proximity of the moon to the earth during early times. These forces exerted by the moon could be substantial enough to have caused events referred to in the creation, such as the division of the firmament from the waters and the gathering of the waters to cause dry land to appear. This deceleration and acceleration of the earth's rotation about its axis could also contribute to the mechanism by which reckoning of time could be changed from the Lord's to man's current time frame. Latter-day Saints are blessed to have scripture that confirm the truth deduced from science. There are neither inconsistencies nor incompatibilities, but only coalescence of truth from either revealed scripture or science.

Abraham 3:3 reveals that a great star named Kolob is closest to the throne of God. Verse 4 further instructs that "Kolob was after the manner of the Lord, according to its times and seasons in the revolutions thereof; that one revolution was a day unto the Lord, after his manner of reckoning, it being one thousand years according to the time appointed unto that whereon thou standest." Thus, when a specific day of the Lord is referenced, then one thousand years of earth time transpires. We cannot be certain that the reference to one thousand years was exact or was meant generically to reflect a long period of time.

This revelation by Abraham was most remarkable for its time. Abraham lived thousands of years before Christ and the prevailing philosophy of his time was that the earth was flat and that the sun rotated around the earth to give rise to day and night. In stark contrast to the teachings of his time, Abraham refers to a day as the time required for the revolution of the planet in which the observer stands. This concept of revolution for a planet infers a spherical shape that rotates around an axis. This is truly a modern concept that was revealed anciently to Abraham. We can also deduce further information from the specifics provided by Abraham. The planet that God dwells on requires one thousand earth years for one complete revolution which constitutes the definition of one day according to Abraham. The planet God dwells on is either huge and takes one thousand earth years to make a complete single rotation or it rotates very slowly.

Abraham 5:13 tells us that, prior to the fall in the Garden of Eden, time was reckoned after the Lord's time. "I, Abraham, saw that it was after the Lord's time, which was after the time of Kolob; for as yet the Gods had not appointed unto Adam his reckoning." There is no indication from the geological history that the earth has drastically changed size. A possible conclusion is that the earth changed its rate of rotation about its axis. Prior to the fall of Adam, the rotation may have been very slow with one rotation every one thousand years. After the fall, the rotation of the earth may have been speeded up to our current rate of one rotation in twenty-four hours.

Current scientific knowledge from astrophysics provides an example for changes in the rotational rate of the earth's ancient history. The moon was once much closer to the earth than it is now. Early in its history, the moon has been estimated to have been only about ten thousand miles from the earth compared to its current average distance of 238,857 miles. The moon's orbit around the earth is becoming larger as time passes.

The position of the moon relative to the earth has great consequences. The moon's gravity pulls on the earth and its large bodies of water and result in earth's oceanic tides. The moon's gravity pulls up the water directly below the moon, and on the other side of the earth, the moon pulls the solid body of the earth away from the water. As a result, two bulges called high tides are formed on the oceans and seas. As the earth turns, these tidal bulges travel from east to west. Every place along the seashore has two high tides and two low tides daily. In the early history of the earth and moon, these gravitational forces may have been huge due to the close proximity of the moon.

These forces could be significant enough to have at least partially contributed to the types of changes referred to in the scriptural creation where the firmament was divided from the waters and waters were gathered together to cause dry land to appear. The resulting tides caused by the near proximity of the moon would be expected to be exaggerated and possibly have drastic effects on the rotational spin of the earth in agreement with the principle of conservation of angular momentum.

An illustration of this principle is provided by the spinning of a figure skater. As a skater spins, their speed is altered by the position of their hands to the body. The angular speed of the skater increases as the hands are moved close to the trunk of the body and conversely slows as the hands are extended outward from the body. In a similar fashion, the moon distorts the spherical shape of the earth due to gravitational forces which then alters the spin rate of the earth. This effect would be dependent on the distance of the moon from the earth, because the gravitational pull by the moon would be directly related to distance. The speed of the earth's spin would slow down as the moon drew closer and speed up as the moon increases its distance from the earth. This deceleration and acceleration of the earth's rotation about its axis could explain at least one possible mechanism by which the reckoning of time could be changed from the Lord's to man's current time frame.

Our solar system contains many examples of planets with altered spin rates. The current speed of the moon's rotation provides an example of different spin rates for planets. The moon revolves around its axis at a very slow rate, one rotation in 29.5 earth days. This lunar day is divided into about two weeks of light and about two weeks of darkness. This slow rotation of the moon results in the ability to observe only one side of the moon, the near side. The far side (the dark side) of the moon was not visualized by man and was a mystery until October 7, 1959, when a Soviet rocket orbited the moon and sent back a few pictures of a portion of the far side. On December 24, 1968, the Apollo 8 astronauts became the first people to directly see the far side. Within our own solar system there is further evidence of different rates of rotation for the planets. Jupiter, which is 318 times the mass of earth (11.2 times in diameter) makes a complete revolution every ten hours. Venus is approximately the same size as earth but revolves much slower, in about 243 earth days.

An additional conclusion from this seminal verse (Abraham 5:13) is the period of time relating to the pre-fall Garden of Eden era was considerable. During this era, Adam reckoned time according to that of the Lord's. This extended time period for the pre-Fall era provides further scriptural evidence for the old age of the earth. The alteration in the speed of revolution of the earth did not distort time, but only altered the calendar or the accounting of time. For example, a day as we know it today had a much longer duration before the fall of Adam.

A revelation regarding the reckoning of time was given to Joseph Smith on April 2, 1843, is recorded in section 130 of the Doctrine and Covenants and provides remarkable insight for the era of time. Verse 4 says, "God's time, angel's time, prophet's time, and man's time, according to the planet on which they reside." This scripture prophetically describes the accounting of time differed from planet to planet. The accounting of time corresponding to a day and night for a spherical planet is dependent on the length of time for a complete rotation about its axis. In 1843, modern astronomy had not revealed that planets had different rates of axial rotation. To declare so boldly that time or planetary spin was different amongst the planets was revolutionary for its time and is further verification of the divine inspiration pertaining to the revelations given to the prophet Joseph Smith.

Chapter Nine

Ancient Earth

Modern scientific technology has provided our generation with evidence for the ancient origin of the earth. Hundreds of reliable scientific tools demonstrate that the earth is billions of years old. These scientific truths are shown to be perfectly consistent with the revealed truth from the scriptures. Science shows the earth had a definite origin referred to as the big bang while the scriptures refer to this event as, "In the beginning." The scriptural narrative of the creation, particularly the book of Abraham, provides ample clues and terminology consistent with the ancient origin of the earth. Substantial scriptural references indicate the seven creation days were long periods of time. For agreement between science and scripture these long creation days must have extended for millions to billions of years. Doctrine and Covenants 77:6 reveals that the age of the temporal earth is seven thousand years old. How can this revelation be reconciled with the ancient age of the earth as determined through scientific evidence? Surprisingly, the answer is quite simple but has been ignored. The earth is seven thousand years old, but the years are reckoned after the Lord's time. Abraham and Peter gave us the key to converting between our time and the Lord's—one thousand years of earth time equals one day unto the Lord. Using this simple conversion factor, the seven thousand-year-old earth according to God years is several billion earth years. In this manner the age of the earth as revealed by God and as determined through science harmonize.

The scientific findings establishing the ancient age of the earth are determined from straightforward principles from physics (nuclear and Newton's laws of gravity), chemistry (thermodynamics and gas laws), and mathematics (vector geometry and calculus). Let us consider three of the most significant scientific evidences for the age dating of the universe. The reality check for the validity of these sciences is obtained from the modern successes achieved in nuclear energy and space travel.

1. Expansion of the universe—Astronomers have measured the motion, direction, and speed of galaxies and found that the universe is expanding outward from a common starting point in space and time. Knowing the distance of these galaxies and their

velocities, the time for their expansion, or the date of the original big bang, can be calculated (i.e., velocity = distance / time). You may have solved similar problems to this in your high school algebra class—if two trains started out at the same time and place and travel at given speeds and for a given time, at what time did they start? The more measurements for the velocities and distances of galaxies the more accurate the calculation. The latest measurements are accurate to approximately 15 percent.

2. Stellar burning—The color and brightness of a star reveals how long it has been burning. The star composition is known to be primarily hydrogen and helium, the mass can be accurately determined, and the burning mechanism of nuclear fusion is well understood, which makes stellar burning the most accurate indicator of the age of the universe. The latest estimates are precise to within approximately 5 percent.

3. Decay of radioactive elements—Supernovae are giant stars in their final explosive stages of burning. The only natural objects in the universe with enough energy sufficient to produce radioactive elements heavier than iron are supernovae. A burst of supernova activity occurred early in the history of the universe but relatively few have occurred since. Radioactive decay proceeds at constant, well-understood rates and all evidence suggests

this constancy extends for over billions of years for some elements. The abundance of radioactive elements provides an estimate of how much time has transpired since the origin of the radioactive element and thereby acts as a miniature atomic clock. Since the origin of radioactive elements correspond to the burst of supernova activity early in the history of the universe, the age of both can be determined. We know the universe cannot be older than a certain age because some radioactive elements still exist. Yet, the universe cannot be very young because considerable radioactive elements have decayed.

All three of these diverse methods converge on a very similar time for the beginning of [illegible]erse of about seventeen (plus or [illegible]ee) billion years ago. A California [illegible] of Technology physicist and Nobel Laureate, Murray Gell-Mann has said, "it would be easier to believe in a flat earth than to believe the universe is 6,000 years old, or anything other than about 15 billion years old." Hugh Ross has more thoroughly reviewed these concepts and please refer to his work for more details on this subject (Ross, 1994, 91–102).

The earth is somewhat younger than the universe. The history of earth is recorded in the rocks of its crust. Rocks have been forming, wearing away, and re-forming ever since the earth took shape. Sediment forms as a product of weathering and erosion and accumulates in layers known as strata. Strata contain clues that tell geologists about earth's past. These clues include the composition of the sediment, the way the strata are deposited, and kinds of fossils that occur in the rock. Scientists have determined that the earth formed about the same time as the rest of our solar system. Chondrite meterorites, the unaltered remains from the formation of the solar system, date back to about the same age as the earth. As described previously, the age of the earth can be determined from measurements of the amounts of natural radioactive materials, such as uranium. Uranium decays into lead at known constant rates. The age of rocks can be determined by comparing the amounts of uranium to the amounts of lead. Such measurements establish the age of the earth to be about 4.6 billion years.

The scriptural accounts of the creation do not provide any specific dates or associated time for these events. However, the narrative provides ample clues and consistent terminology with the ancient origin of the earth. For reconciliation of these scientific truths with the revealed scriptures, first and foremost one must accept that the seven creation days described in Genesis actually refer to long periods, times, eras, or epochs, some of which extended for millions to billions of years. Abraham clearly and repetitively refers to "creation times" rather than days. Abraham also uses phrases such as "brooding," "prepare the earth to bring forth," "prepare the waters to bring forth," and "Gods took council," which all infer time-dependent processes.

Long creation periods are inferred from the seventh creation time. Each of the six previous creation times was specifically divided into a morning and an evening. The morning and evening signifies a beginning and end for a creation period rather than the specific time associated with the rising and setting of the sun. However, on the seventh creation time they rested from their labors and made no mention of a morning and an evening. The consistent mention of a morning and an evening for each of the six creation times and the distinct absence from the seventh period is a strong message that this period has not ended. The seventh creation time is still ongoing. The scriptures (Ps. 95:7–11; John 5:16–18; Heb. 4:1–11) reinforce the continuation through the present and extenuation into the future of the seventh creation time or period of rest. The seventh creation period, or rest from the creation, will end as referred to in Revelation 21, when evil is ultimately conquered and "all things will be made new" and "all former things are passed away."

The extension of the seventh creation day from Adam until modern day is a substantial example that the creation days are really long, extended periods of time. The rest that God refers to concerning the seventh creation period does not literally mean a rest from all work, for God is very busy dealing with current human affairs—Doctrine and Covenants 84:80 says, "a hair of his head shall not fall . . . unnoticed." Instead, God refers to a rest from creating new species and life forms for the planet earth.

The cessation from divine creative activities is most evident from the fossil record, new life forms proliferated prior to the creation of man. Frequent extinctions have occurred since the ancient past and continue today, but the introduction rate of new species is nil. The scriptures offer an explanation for the sudden change in the rate of speciation, the Gods changed the level of their creative activity after the sixth creation time.

An additional clue to the meaning of day used in Genesis comes from the understanding of the differences between Hebrew and English. The original language of the Old Testament was Hebrew and has since been translated numerous times into English. Sometimes the difference between the languages results in translation deficiencies. Hebrew vocabulary is limited in size, almost a thousand times smaller than English. Most Hebrew words have several meanings that are easily misconstrued when interpreted into English. The Hebrew word *yôm* literally means a twenty-four-hour period, or any long but definite period of time. In Biblical Hebrew, no other word carries the meaning of a long period of time, whereas in English we have multiple choices for a word to denote long periods of time: *epoch, era, age,* etc. Like Hebrew, the word *day* also has multiple meanings in English. *Day* could refer to a twenty-four-hour period of time or to the figurative usage such as the day of the Egyptians and the day of the dark ages, meaning a period of time. The translation of the Hebrew word *yôm* in Genesis to English could have benefited by the choice of the word *era, time,* or *period* rather than *day* (Ross, 1994, 46–47). Joseph Smith in his inspired translation of the creation in the book of Abraham did repetitively choose the word *time* when referring to the creation periods. There should be no confusion that the creation times or days mentioned in the scriptures lasted for long periods of time (millions to billions of our years) and were not twenty-four hours long.

Abraham provides profound scriptural insight pertinent to the ancient age of the earth. Abraham 5:13 tells us that prior to the fall in the Garden of Eden, time was reckoned after the Lord's time. "I, Abraham, saw that it was after the Lord's time . . . for as yet the Gods had not appointed unto Adam his reckoning." Prior to the fall of Adam, time was reckoned according to the Lord's reckoning. Joseph Smith received further revelation regarding the reckoning of time in section 130 of the Doctrine and Covenants, and provides remarkable insight for the era of time. Verse 4 says, "God's time, angel's time, prophet's time, and man's time" are all different and is "according to the planet on which they reside." This scripture prophetically describes that the accounting of time differs between God and man. Man's perspective of time is prejudiced by a finite beginning and end of a typical lifespan on earth. God's perspective of time is much different, he has neither beginning nor end, he is infinite and eternal, from everlasting to everlasting. As such, the long creation periods of millions to billions of earth years may seem colossal to us but may be but a short time on God's time frame.

The scriptures provide a glimpse into God's time reckoning. 2 Peter 3 is reflecting on the history of the earth and the Second Coming tells us, "But beloved, be not ignorant of this one thing, that one day is with the Lord as a thousand years." Abraham received a revelation concerning the reckoning of the Lord's time, and of a great star named Kolob that is closest to the throne of God. Abraham 3:4 declares "that Kolob was after the manner of the Lord, according to its times and seasons in the revolutions thereof: that one revolution was a day unto the Lord, after his manner of reckoning, it being one thousand years according to the time appointed unto that whereon thou standest. This is the reckoning of the Lord's time."

The prophet Joseph Smith received further revelation concerning the explanation of the book of Revelation that is related to this topic of time. Doctrine and Covenants 77:6 says, "What are we to understand by the book which John saw, which was sealed on the back with seven seals? We are to understand that it contains the revealed will, mysteries, and the works of God: the hidden things of his economy concerning this earth during the seven thousand years of its continuance, or its temporal existence."

This is telling us that the temporal existence of the earth is seven thousand years. Many have interpreted this to indicate that the earth is only seven thousand years old, which is totally inconsistent with known facts from modern science. This apparent difference has unnecessarily created an enormous chasm between religion and science, to the point that each may ignore the other. How can this apparent difference be reconciled? Surprisingly, the answer is quite simple and has been ignored. Hebrews 6:18 tells us that "it is impossible for God to lie." The simple answer is as God has told us, the earth is seven thousand years old, but the years are in the Lord's time after his reckoning.

Using simple math and the key conversion factor provided in the scriptures of 1 Lord's day = 1,000 earth years the earth may be calculated to be 2.6 billion years old. For example, age of the earth = 7,000 God years x (365 God days / 1 God year) x (1000 earth years / 1 God day) = 2,555,000,000 earth years. All scientific evidence shows the earth to be 4–5 billion years old. From a first approximation, these two dates, 2.6 billion versus 4–5 billion years, are similar, that is they have the same order of magnitude.

The deduced date of 2.6 billion years required an assumption based on the analogy of earth, that 1 of God's years = 365 of God's days. We determine a year by the time required for the earth to orbit around our sun.

In Abraham's vision we are told somewhat concerning this, "And I saw the stars, that they were very great, and that one of them was nearest unto the throne of God . . . And the Lord said . . . the name of the great one is Kolob, because it is near unto me . . . I have set this one to govern all those which belong to the same order" (3:2–3). Apparently, the planet in which the throne of God dwells orbits around the great sun, named Kolob. If this orbit around Kolob takes twice as long as our year, then the age of the earth determined from science and the scriptures perfectly match.

Chapter Ten

Adam Was the First Human

The scriptures are unambiguous in stating that Adam was the first human on earth. Scientific evidence, including extrapolations from DNA mutational rates, and religious artifacts and other examples of religious worship date the origin of true humans to thirty thousand plus or minus fifteen thousand years ago. Recent anthropological and molecular biological evidence definitively establish that one group of ape-like primates, referred to as Neanderthals that had large brains, walked upright, and predated humans, cannot be the predecessors to humans. Some have interpreted the genealogies provided in the Bible to indicate Adam lived about six thousand years ago, which is not consistent with the known earlier existence of humans that worshiped a supreme deity. Hebrew scholars and careful scrutiny shows the Biblical genealogy to be noncontiguous with significant gaps. Such skipped generations place the age of Adam to be consistent with the historical evidence for the origin of humans.

At the end of the sixth creation period "the Gods went down to organize man in their own image, in the image of the Gods to form they them, male and female to form they them" (Abr, 3:27). Moses 1:34 states, "And the first man of all men have I called Adam, which is many." Adam's name signifies "many" and pertains to the greatness of his posterity that would follow him. The other scriptural accounts of the creation including statements in 1 Nephi 5:11 and Doctrine and Covenants 84:16 are clear and unequivocal that Adam was the first man upon the earth.

Many Hebrew scholars place the creation of Adam and Eve to be about ten thousand to thirty-five thousand years ago. This period of time agrees very well with the archaeological derived date for the existence of humans that had the capacity to worship a Supreme Being. Religious relics and remains of altars for worship have been found that date back between eight thousand to twenty-four thousand years ago. Primates referred to as hominids that had large brains, walked upright, and used tools roamed the earth as long ago as one million years. These hominids were not humans despite that they buried their dead and painted pictures of animals on cave walls. Modern bower birds, zebra finches, elephants, chimpanzees, and gorillas engage in similar activities to a limited extent.

The defining feature of humans, created after the image of God, is the capability to worship God and to form a relationship with him. The remains of altars, temples, and various religious relics are the evidence of worship. Hominids may have been intelligent mammals but they were not humans nor did Adam descend from them.

Emerging evidence from anthropology indicates that the hominids had gone extinct before the appearance of humans. Recent evidence from anatomical anthropology and biochemistry provide conclusive evidence that a subclass of hominids known as Neandertals could not have contributed to the human gene pool.

Distinguished American anthropologists as recently as 1996 measured the nasal characteristics of thirteen different Neandertal skulls kept in museums around the world. They discovered that Neandertals possessed enormous nasal bones and huge sinus cavities compared to modern humans, and had no tear ducts. Based on morphology, they concluded that Neandertals cannot be direct predecesors to humans or any known primates (Schwartz & Tattersall, 1996; Laitman et al., 1996). Just as modern humans appear to have been specially created, so too were Neanderthals.

Recent advances in biochemistry corroborate the conclusion that the human race is not descended from the Neandertals. In 1997, DNA samples were successfully extracted from the skeleton of the first Neandertal ever found in a limestone quarry in Neandertal, Germany in 1856. A DNA fragment 379-nucleotide-pairs long was conclusively determined for the Neandertals mitochondrial DNA. The Neandertal DNA fragment was compared with DNA strands of 986 nucleotide pairs from living humans of diverse ethnic backgrounds. The difference was extensive with an average of twenty-six different nucleotide bases. The diverse modern human gene pool differed from each another by only eight bases and were independent from the twenty-six of the Neandertals. The researchers definitively concluded that Neandertals have not contributed to the human gene pool (Whitfield et al., 1995). Many other groups of hominids have been discovered. But details concerning their genetic origins have not been reported. Thus, conclusions concerning their ancestry cannot be drawn at this time.

Additional recent scientific studies can be nicely explained through a Biblical origin. The natural rate of DNA mutation was determined. By knowing the diversity of DNA throughout modern humans and using the natural rate of mutation, the approximate elapsed time since the first human couple can be estimated. This estimate can be done for males and females separately. This is possible because only males carry the Y chromosome and receive the corresponding DNA from their fathers only, while DNA from mitochondria (specialized energy-producing cell organelles) is almost exclusively inherited from mothers only. The interesting conclusion from these studies is that the original common ancestor for all human males dates somewhere between 35,000 to 47,000 B.C. Whereas, the research placed the common ancestor of all women somewhere between a few thousand to ten thousand years earlier.

The Bible provides a rational explanation for the earlier origin of women (Ross, 1998, 110–112). The events of the flood during Noah's era reveal why the most recent common ancestor of all women predate the most recent common ancestor of all men. Of the eight people on board Noah's ark, the four men were blood-related but not the four women. The most recent common ancestor for the four men on the ark, and all men since, was Noah. The most recent common ancestor for the four women on the ark, Noah's wife and daughters-in-law (nonblood related relatives) was Eve. The difference in the biochemical derived dates for female and male roughly fits the time frame difference between Eve and Noah.

A separate conclusion can be determined from the estimated date for the origin of humans from the DNA mutational rate. The bipedal primate hominids were long extinct before the first humans and could therefore not be related.

The dates approximated by mutational rates of DNA are only approximate and rough estimates. They rely on relatively small population samples and relatively small numbers of nucleotide base pairs. As more data is accumulated these estimates may get refined.

Some Biblical genealogist have suggested that Adam and Eve lived about six thousand years ago. This does not coincide with the abundant archeological evidence for an earlier presence of God-fearing humans. The six-thousand-year-old suggestion is based on the assumption that no generations were omitted from the Biblical genealogy and that the years referred to in the text were equal to 365 days. Hebrew genealogies tend to focus on their heroes or most notable characters. Therefore, gaps may be expected.

A careful examination of the Hebrew words used in the Biblical genealogy provides an important perspective. The Hebrew words used for *father* and *son, ab* and *ben,* have broader definitions than the English translations indicate. *Ab* sometimes refers to grandfather, great-grandfather, or great-great-grandfather, etc. Similarly, *ben* can mean son, great-grandson, etc. In the English translation from Hebrew, complete generations could easily be skipped due to the ambiguity of *ab* and *ben*. Examples from the Bible further illustrate this point. In the book of Daniel, Belshazzar's mother refers to Nebuchadnezzar as her son's father though, in fact, two kings separated them (Ross, 1998, 108–110). A careful comparison of parallel genealogies in 1 Chronicles 3 and Matthew 1 disagree with one another. Matthew left out three generations that were mentioned in the parallel genealogy in Chronicles. Even in the genealogies of Genesis 5 and 11, where the years between the birthdates of the father and son were provided, do not agree with that in Luke 3. For example, Luke 3 inserts at least one generation, namely Cainan, between Shelah and Arphaxad, while Genesis 11 records Shelah as the son of Arphaxad.

Bible scholars provide a reasonable explanation for the omission of certain descendants. Hebrew writing is full of cadence and patterns that hold symbolic importance. In the genealogy provided in Matthew, three groups of fourteen generations each are listed. The first fourteen generations included Abraham to David, the second fourteen were composed of David to the Babylonian exile, and the third set of fourteen from the Babylonian exile to Jesus. To maintain the pattern of three sets of fourteen descendants, less significant names were dropped. The existence of gaps in the genealogy cause these lists to be considered as adequate but should not be construed as complete. Thus, the reason to strictly adhere to the six-thousand-year-old assumption for the age of Adam is without warrant.

Chapter Eleven

Vestigial Structures and Fossils

A vestigial (degenerate) appendage from the serpent family provides a most amazing artifact from the Garden of Eden. Certain snakes possess a vestigial limb bone indicating that they were once limbed animals. The scriptures reveal the explanation. The serpent that beguiled Eve was cursed thereafter to crawl upon its belly. Subsequently, the serpent and its progeny lost its limbs. The vestigial limb bones of today may be a remnant of the once limbed serpent that were lost due to God's invoked curse. Other examples of vestigial structures come from temporary "animal-like" characteristics observed during human embryonic development. This astonishing process is a marvelous reflection of divine engineering. The concept of creation according to a common design and the realization of the common thread used by the ultimate design engineer (God) nicely clarify these examples of vestigial structures.

Nature's best historical relics, fossils, provide a spectacular correlation to the scriptural account of the creation. The fossil record documents amazing creatures that once lived but have since become extinct. These extinct life forms filled important niches at the time of their existence and contributed significantly to the development and preparation of earth. These extinct organisms were created specifically for a distinct purpose and played a role that modern species could not. Many other kinds of fossilized life forms are similar to existing organisms today and appear in the fossil sequence abruptly and distinctly, then show minor variation in their type over time. The fossil record shows that fossils are not found at random. They are found in groups or geographical systems with an apparent progression of life forms from simple to more complex as time progressed. The sudden appearance of species and the sequence of their introduction over time accurately mirror the creation phases described in the scriptures. The fossil record faithfully shows that historical life forms fit into distinct classes or species with no evidence of transitional states between species. The lack of intermediate forms suggests a general law, like begets like. The scriptural account of the creation described this law long before the first fossil was discovered. After the creation of each life form, the Gods specifically commanded them to reproduce after their kind.

Vestigial Structures

Vestigial or *vestige* refers to a trace, mark, or visible sign left by something vanished or lost. For example, a ruin or artifact from an ancient city is considered a vestige. In biology, vestigial is used to connote a bodily part or organ that is small and degenerate or imperfectly developed in comparison to one or more fully developed in an earlier stage of an individual, in a past generation, or in a closely related form. The human appendix is frequently sited as a vestigial organ, with no modern function.

A vestigial appendage from the reptile family provides a most amazing artifact from the Garden of Eden. Certain snakes possess a vestigial limb bone indicating that they were once limbed animals. Moses 4:20 and Genesis 3:14 state that the serpent that beguiled Eve into partaking of the tree of knowledge of good and evil was "cursed above all cattle, and above every beast of the field; upon thy belly shalt thou go, and dust shalt thou eat all the days of thy life." By logical deduction, the snake prior to being cursed did not crawl upon its belly but had legs or similar appendages for mobility. After the fall, the snake and its progeny lost their limbs and were destined to slither upon their stomach.

The vestigial limb bones found today may be a remnant and a natural consequence of the mechanism by which the Lord invoked the curse. The two scriptural records have identical wording with regard to this account and give added credence and validity to the reality of this event. Surely, this is not a coincidence—that the serpent was involved in the fall, the curse of lost limbs, and the vestigial appendages in modern snakes. The recognition of vestigial limbs in snakes is a modern anatomical observation of which Moses most likely was unaware. This appears to be a newly unearthed gem that has been discovered by modern science and is waiting to be recognized as a further testament of the reality of the creation story as recorded in the scriptures.

There are other examples of vestigial organs, particularly with regard to embryonic development (Morris and Parker, 1987, 61–68). The astonishing process by which fetal humans develop is a marvelous reflection of divine engineering. Human embryos develop through a series of stages, some of which contain temporary animal-like characteristics that some have interpreted as vestigial structures. For example, the fetus at about one month has a yolk sac that resembles a chicken, a tail like a lizard, and gill slits like a fish. Careful examination of each specific case reveals the design of a single creator. As with any engineer, the creator of life has used a common design to construct the bodies of animal life. Certain structures and processes are optimal and were used repeatedly. Thus, similarities and common features can easily be observed throughout the animal kingdom. The human arm has bones inside—a single upper bone attached to the shoulder, two bones in the forearm—a group of smaller bones making up the wrist, and bones that project out into fingers. Many other animals have a similar pattern, the foreleg of a horse, or dog, the wing of a bat, and the flipper of a penguin. Biologists use the term *homology* for such similarities in structure. Such examples of homology are nicely understood by the concept of creation according to a common design. The examples of vestigial structures can best be appreciated by realization of the common thread used by the ultimate design engineer.

The apparent human embryonic yolk sac has a vague resemblance to the yolk of chicken eggs, but has a completely different function. In chickens, the yolk contains much of the food that the chick depends on for growth. In humans this nourishment comes from the mother by attachment through the umbilical cord. The so-called human yolk sac is the source of the embryo's first blood cells. The human embryo must generate its own blood cells because they are not maternally derived. After birth the blood cells are derived from stem cells within the marrow of bones. These stem cells receive chemical signals from the body to mature into the many different types of blood cells such as lymphocytes, neutrophils, platelets, etc., depending on the body's needs. These stem cells are very sensitive to mutation by natural radiation and are protected by the surrounding bone. Bone marrow needs a blood supply to be formed and the early embryo faces a dilemma because it has neither well-developed bone nor blood. Where does the blood first come from?

Apparently the Creator has solved the embryo's dilemma by utilizing a structure similar to the yolk sac in chickens. After all, the DNA, protein, lipids, and other cellular components for making the human embryo yolk sac and the chicks yolk are "common stock" building materials. The human embryo yolk sac is conveniently located externally to the embryo itself and can easily be discarded after it has served its temporary yet vital function.

This scenario of the human embryo's yolk sac is that expected from good creative design and engineering. As an analogy, we can look at the example of great structures built by mankind. The magnificent cathedrals or castles of Europe have certain building features in common. These same features, materials, and parts can be adapted to meet a wide variety of needs. This commonality can be visually observed throughout these edifices. This is particularly obvious for buildings constructed by the same architect or builder. Common themes and the stamp of the originator are apparent. In a similar manner, as we examine the creations of God we should observe common themes, homologies, and the same structures in various species adapted for different purposes. That's what we observe in human embryonic development. The same kind of structures that provide food for the chick can be adapted to provide blood cells to the human embryo.

The same is true of the apparent gill slits. In the one-month-old human embryo, there are wrinkles, grooves, or pouches in the skin in the region of the future throat. These throat features are falsely called gill slits, but they never function as gills. Instead, they develop into essential parts of human anatomy. The middle ear canals come from the second pouches, and the parathyroid and thymus glands come from the third and fourth. As with yolk sacs, the gill slits formation represents an ingenious and adaptable solution to a difficult engineering problem. How can a small egg cell be turned into an animal or human being with a digestive tube and various organs inside a body cavity? The solution by the Creator is to have parts or regions of the early embryo "swallow itself," to form a tube which then "buds off" other tubes and pouches. The anterior pituitary, lungs, urinary bladder, and parts of the liver and pancreas develop by this maneuver. In fish, gills develop from such processes, and in humans, the ear canals, parathyroid, and thymus glands develop. In this manner, fish and humans each use a similar process to develop their distinctive features.

Some have argued that the small tail that appears transiently in human embryos is a useless remnant from our related ancestors that had tails. This embryonic tail is the precursor to the adult tail bone, otherwise known as a coccyx. The coccyx is a very important bone in the body that provides a point of muscle attachment required for an upright posture and even excretion. In the one-month-old embryo, the end of the spine sticks out noticeably. This is because the muscles and limbs don't develop until later. After the legs develop they surround and envelop the coccyx, which ends up inside the body. This is the last example of creation by common design that we will consider, but many others are apparent to the careful observer.

Fossils

Fossils are nature's best relics pertaining to the history of the earth. They are the remains of plants and animals from previous ages that are preserved in the earth's crust. The fossils trapped within the stratified layers of sedimentary rock are of particular interest. Geology has shown these strata represent a successive layering effect with the top representing the most recent layer followed by a successive aging to the oldest layer at the bottom. These sedimentary layers were deposited over millions to billions of years. The fossils trapped within these strata tell a chronological story of God's creations. The fossils within particular strata represent the life forms that were living at the time the strata were formed. The tons of fossils that have been unearthed tell a powerful story that testifies of the divine nature of the creation.

What is this story of the fossil record? Some of the most significant findings are: (1) Amazing creatures have been unearthed for which there are no modern counterparts. The best known of these are the dinosaurs. (2) Many kinds of fossilized life forms appear in the fossil sequence abruptly and distinctly, then show minor variation in their type over time, and finally abruptly disappear. (3) Other fossils are very similar to existing organisms today or represent slight variations that can be classified according to criteria derived from modern life forms. (4) No legitimate missing links or forms that represent transitional or in-between species have been uncovered. (5) Life progressed from simple forms to more complex over time. How do these observations testify of the creator?

Surprisingly, most of God's creations have become extinct. These extinct life forms should not be considered mistakes or examples of a trial and error creation. Abraham 4:26 tells us concerning the creation, "And the Gods took counsel among themselves." Chapter 5:3 further says, "and thus were their decisions at the time that they counseled among themselves to form the heavens and the earth." These verses clearly describe a careful, planned out, and well executed creation. These extinct life forms filled important niches at the time of their existence and contributed significantly to the development and preparation of the earth. These extinct organisms were created specifically for a distinct purpose and played a role that modern species could not.

The formation of petroleum is a good example of how extinct life forms have contributed to the resources of nature. Geologists have learned that petroleum was formed from remains of organisms that died millions of years ago. The organic theory of petroleum formation is based on the presence of certain carbon-containing substances in oil. Such substances could have come only from once-living organisms. Masses of tiny organisms, particularly from the water, and large creatures from the land died and became trapped in sediments. The sediments piled up and buried the organic debris below the surface of land and water. As the sediments became buried deeper they were subjected to increasingly high temperatures and pressures. These conditions caused the organic debris to go through a chemical change that resulted in the formation of oil and natural gas. The narrow temperature range that oil can form is called the oil window, and occurs at about 100°C. At temperatures below this range, little oil forms and at great depths, where temperatures are higher, most oil decomposes.

This process of converting organic matter into oil requires millions of years of the correct conditions of pressure, heat, and bacterial action to form useful amounts of oil. The massive petroleum deposits of today are the lifeblood of industrialized countries. This example of oil formation is what the scriptural account of the creation refers to: "And the gods prepared the earth to bring forth the living creature" and "Let us prepare the waters to bring forth abundantly the moving creatures that have life." When the Gods used the term, "abundantly" they were serious. For example, a glimpse into the scale is provided in the Karoo fossil beds in Africa which contain the remains of perhaps one trillion vertebrates.

Another example is the dinosaurs that lived about two hundred million years ago and became abruptly extinct about one hundred million years ago. Most striking was the large size of some. Many were herbivores while others were ferocious carnivores. The large size of dinosaurs and the abundance of smaller organisms described above contributed to the vast deposits of petroleum needed to fuel the inhabitants of modern earth. Decomposition of their carcasses buried deep under the sediment in massive numbers over millions of years contributed to the rich oil reserves of today. Unburied decomposition of infrequent numbers would not give rise to the needed result.

To optimize the chances of being preserved as a fossil an organism must be rapidly buried under a heavy load of sediment. Otherwise, scavengers and erosion will decompose the specimen with scarcely a trace. Once a plant or animal was buried deeply enough in the right kind of sediment, minerals accumulated in the specimen or in the cavity left by the rotted structure. In this manner, fossils were preserved for future eons with their contemporary environment entombed about them. Mechanisms for massive burial of large populations were necessary. The cold-blooded nature of these reptiles made them vulnerable to sudden extinction due to precipitous changes in temperature. Extremes of climate, earthquakes, volcanoes, flooding, mountain building, glaciating, meteorite collisions, and other similar catastrophes could serve the above purposes. Dinosaurs could not have survived for the requisite time without the appropriate balance of the producer and consumer relationship of herbivores and carnivores. Because of their size, ferocity, and the need for an unstable cataclysmic environment during the preparative era of the earth, dinosaurs did not coexist with modern humans. Thus, once their purpose for the design of the earth had been accomplished they abruptly underwent extinction.

Another major observation from the fossil record is that historical life forms fit into distinct classes or species. In other words, no legitimate fossils have been uncovered that represent transitional states between species. The lack of intermediate forms suggests a general law—like begets like. For example, crocodiles were always crocodiles. The scriptural account of the creation described this law long before the first fossil was discovered. After the creation of each life form, the Gods specifically commanded them to reproduce after their kind. Within a natural setting, all living organisms will fertilize or reproduce within their own species. This may be observed in all current life and is evident from the historic record produced by fossils. An interesting example of this phenomenon is the mule. With some encouragement a mare (female horse) and a male donkey will breed. The resulting offspring is a mule, but it is sterile and incapable of further reproduction.

The Gods did bestow upon all organisms the ability to adapt to changing conditions. This inherent attribute has permitted life to persist according to the great plan of the Gods. The variation of organisms within a species is evident all around us. Many have experienced the change of dandelions or weeds within their lawn from the beginning of spring into summer. As the mowing season matures the dandelions grow closer to the ground and avoid destruction by the mower. This same type of variation within a species has been observed in the fossil record. Each basic type of plant and animal life in the fossil sequence is complete, fully formed, and functional. Each classifies according to the criteria we use to distinguish groups today. Each type shows broad ecological variations within its type, but no complete changes to different species have been documented. However, the absence of fossils from transitional states of species does not prove their nonexistence. Many reasons could explain the scarcity of their fossil remains. But thus far, no direct fossil evidence exist for intermediate states.

The last major conclusion from the fossil record that we will consider is that fossils are not found at random. They are found in groups or geological systems with an apparent progression of life forms from simple to more complex as time progressed. The oldest and simplest fossils were buried deepest within the earth. Most commonly, the complexity increases and the age of fossils decreases nearer the surface. This tendency for fossils to be found in a certain vertical order is known as a geologic column. The geologic column represents different ecological zones, the buried remains of plants and animals that once lived together in the same time period and same environment. The geologic column is conspicuously similar to that expected from the creation events described in the scriptures. The scriptures clearly lay out the creation in six periods of time with the introduction of life forms in a step-by-step manner starting with the simplest to the most complex (see chapter 6).

Chapter Twelve

Evolution

Evolution is the process of change from a simpler to a more complex state, i.e. life was derived from more primitive ancestors through gradual modification in successive generations. The heart of evolution is the concept of survival of the fittest coupled with random genetic mutation. Over long periods of time, change was introduced through mutations and the screen of natural selection used for evolution. The description of the creation in the scriptures is strikingly consistent with the main tenet of evolution. Species appeared gradually over long periods of time beginning with simple and progressing to more complex organisms. The Gods endowed living species with the resilience to adapt to changing environments. The details of this resilience have been elucidated by modern molecular biology and lie within the ability of the DNA molecule to change.

Science has discovered how to manipulate and engineer the DNA molecule within the laboratory. Exact replicas of animals can be created through the laboratory process of cloning. Primordial cells referred to as "stem cells" can be enticed to develop into a variety of specialized cells with critical life-sustaining functions. Medical research is perhaps uncovering the details of how the Gods created the diversity of species.

The scriptures are incontrovertible—the Gods were intimately involved with the creation. The Gods planned, counseled, made decisions, watched, brooded, and even directly visited the earth from time to time to bring to pass the introduction of species. A divinely engineered creation is described, wherein the Gods utilized a combination of all the mechanisms discovered by science, such as random genetic mutation, natural selection, and direct intervention by visits to the earth to perhaps perform genetic manipulations.

The theory of evolution stimulates diverse reactions from people. Evolution is the process of change from a simpler or worse to a more complex or better state. With regard to the creation, this infers that the wide array of flora and fauna are in part derived from more primitive ancestors through a gradual modification in successive generations. The negative response that many Christians have toward evolution is due to the over-zealous interpretation of some scientists that the entire origin of species resulted from an evolutionary process in the total absence of God. The scriptures are absolute; the Gods were intimately involved with the creation. The Gods planned, counseled, made decisions, watched, brooded, and even directly visited the earth from time to time to bring to pass the introduction of species. However, the scriptures provide no information regarding the mechanism by which diversity originated. This dearth leaves considerable latitude for the latter-day saint to formulate varied opinions on how the creation developed. Providing that God's involvement in the creation is adequately acknowledged, we should feel unencumbered to devise the most rational opinion possible. This opinion should be dynamic and adaptive to new discoveries of truth.

The creation process described in the scriptures as elaborated in the preceding chapters of this book is strikingly consistent with the main tenet of evolution. Species appeared gradually over long periods of time beginning with simple and progressing to more complex organisms. The discoveries of evolutionary science provide considerable insight into possible details of how the Gods accomplished the introduction of species. God provided a framework description of the creation in the scriptures and science is discovering the details of how.

The heart of evolution is the concept of survival of the fittest coupled with random genetic mutation. Pressure from competition for limited food and resources results in the elimination of the weaker population of living organisms while the stronger thrive, preferentially reproduce, and contribute their characteristics to their progeny. Many external and internal factors induce random mutations in the genetic blueprint of living organisms. Some mutations are deleterious yet others are adventitious. Over time, change is introduced and the screen of natural selection picks and chooses for evolution. In this manner, through millions of years of the earth's history some of the diversity of living organisms may have been introduced. The common peppered moth of England provides an astounding example of the property of natural selection.

For over a century, two varieties of the peppered moth have existed. One form is light-colored with small dark spots irregularly scattered over its wings and body. The other, is much darker due to the presence of the pigment melanin and is often called the "melanic" form. In the past, the light form was more common than the dark. The light form was protectively colored in the biological counterpart of military camouflage. This protective coloring is an inherited pattern of pigmentation, which allowed them to blend in with their backgrounds. On tree trunks covered with lichens, light varieties of the peppered moth are perfectly camouflaged, but the darker form stands out prominently. The dark form was more subject to predation by birds than the light form.

Nevertheless, in the past hundred years the number of melanic moths has increased quite drastically. In some areas the dark form has totally replaced the light. The dark form now predominates in the industrial centers and the regions to the southeast. Investigation of these regions shows that the smoke and soot from factories has significantly darkened the natural background of these regions. In addition, prevailing southwesterly winds have deposited soot in the eastern regions. On a darker background, the light-colored moths that had previously been well camouflaged became more visible. As a result, these light varieties became subject to greater predation from birds. The number of light-colored moths able to reach maturity and reproduce decreased proportionately. The genes for light color consequently reached fewer members of the next generation. The melanic form of the peppered moth arose originally by a mutation of the gene controlling coloration. This mutation was disadvantageous on the original, light-colored background, and natural selection was unfavorable to it. However, through the change in the environment due to industrial growth, the mutant was favored. The result was that the melanic genes spread through the population. At the present time the melanic form has completely replaced the lighter form in certain areas, indicating the greater selective advantage.

Many other similar examples of natural selection have been documented and thoroughly studied by modern genetic analysis. The Gods endowed all organisms with the resilience to adapt to changing environments. The details of this resilience lie within the DNA that composes the genetic blueprint. Throughout the life span of an organism the DNA is continuously being replicated and subject to random mutation. The fidelity of this DNA replication is amazingly true, but infrequent variations do occur. These infrequent variations bestow organisms with the ability to change and adapt to varying environmental conditions.

Viruses are microbes that have specialized in the ability to mutate and thus survive. Viruses are incapable of surviving on their own. They invade cells of other organisms and trick their host into supporting growth of new viruses. The host cells have adopted many defense strategies to ward off such virus invasions. On the other hand, viruses mutate so rapidly that they stay one step ahead of their host cell defenses. As a result, viruses are ancient and have flourished causing infectious diseases on plants, animals, and humans.

The ability for organisms to mutate, evolve, and adapt to changing environmental pressures is uncontestable. The pertinent questions regarding the creation are the following: Can this phenomenon of mutation and natural selection lead to the formation of new species? Could this be the mechanism by which God created the diversity of organic life? Modern science has clearly identified that genetic mutation coupled with natural selection is a powerful force that may have been used by the Gods to help create diversity. This process is based on known principles of biochemistry that have partially been duplicated in the laboratory.

There is every reason to embrace and welcome the truths uncovered by evolutionary science. The scriptural description of the creation provides further support. Regarding the creatures of the ocean and land, Abraham 4:20, 24–25 says, "Let us prepare the waters to bring forth abundantly the moving creatures. . . . And the Gods prepared the earth to bring forth the living creature . . . And the Gods organized the earth to bring forth the beast." These scriptures paint the following reasonable scenario; the Gods prepared and organized the water and earth in such a manner that the water and earth subsequently brought forth the abundance of creatures, suggesting the Gods utilized an orchestrated evolutionary-type process to help populate life on earth. This creation mechanism of mutation and natural selection may have been used to some extent by the Gods, but not exclusively. Divine intervention was necessary. Such a scenario is very consistent with the discoveries of evolutionary science.

A remaining question is how frequently did the Gods intervene? The scriptures describe a creation in which the Gods intervened, for they carefully planned, prepared, organized, made decisions, and visited the earth directly. The frequency of their intervention has not been revealed nor discovered by scientific investigation. There is much room for varied opinion and personal preference on this matter.

Recent advances in the life sciences may reveal clues to the activities of the Gods during their creation visits to the earth, and in particular how new species may have been created. The secrets for manipulation of genetic material have been discovered in our generation. DNA can be dissembled, reassembled, cut, spliced, synthesized, exaggerated, inserted into foreign cells, and made to function at will. A cell can be depleted of its genetic material, the DNA from another can be introduced, and the hybrid cell can be induced to develop into a complete organism with the exact genetic replica of the latter. This process is referred to as cloning. Numerous animals have been cloned and human cloning appears imminent.

Thus far, cloning of a complete organism has only been achieved when the host cell and introduced DNA remains within the same species. But it is reasonable to imagine that cloning between species may be possible.

Cells within organisms have developed specialized functions. Humans have cells that function as liver, heart, kidney, and etc. However, certain primary cells exist that have not yet differentiated into their specialized functions. These are referred to as "stem cells" and serve as a reservoir and are capable of developing into many different types of specialized cells. Scientists have unlocked the biochemical signals that instruct these stem cells to differentiate into various mature functions. With proper laboratory conditions stem cells can be induced to grow into replacement tissues and organs for donor purposes. These processes are clearly God-like capabilities that are being conducted in laboratories throughout the world. Perhaps when the Gods visited the earth to create new species and endow organisms with new functions they performed procedures that have some resemblance to current methods of cloning and stem cell technology. Visits to the earth by the Gods for the purpose of conducting divine engineering was necessary. The Gods could have utilized all the tools of direct genetic engineering, random mutation, and natural selection to accomplish the creation. Modern science is unlocking the mysteries of how the Gods created the diversity of life.

The resurrection is a process related to creation in which the modern advances of cloning are equally pertinent. Latter-day saint revelation concerning resurrection describes the literal bringing forth of our physical bodies to join with our spirits. Moroni 10:34 testifies concerning the resurrection, "I soon go to rest in the paradise of God, until my spirit and body shall again reunite." Many reject the possibility of a literal resurrection because it seems impossible to restore that which has returned to the dust of the earth. Human cloning brings a reality and an explanation for how the resurrection could be accomplished. Every cell of the human body contains the complete genetic blueprint for the entire person. In the process of cloning an exact replica of our physical bodies is created. Scientists have found copies of this blueprint still intact in bodies that have been buried for hundreds of years. It doesn't take any science fiction at all to imagine duplicating an exact physical replica from such a single copy of this blueprint. If man can achieve such feats as we are seeing in modern science, why can't God, the greatest scientist of all, make the resurrection of all mankind a reality?

Chapter Thirteen

Conclusion

The earth was created through the process of divine engineering. The Gods used a process of common design, gene manipulation, and optimal biochemistry for the creation of diverse life forms. A careful examination of the scriptural versions of the creation is fully consistent with veritable evidence from modern science. Even from the earliest known event there is harmony. The first reported entity or matter from both the scriptures and science was light. Science uses terms such as big bang, electromagnetic radiation, photon, and matter/antimatter while the scriptures and prophets similarly refer to the terms chaos, intelligences, light of truth, glory, and spirit matter.

Reasonable interpretations of latter-day scriptures establish the temporal age of the earth to be billions of years old. The ancient age of the earth is fundamental to the harmonious agreement between religion and science. The extreme age of the earth was necessary for its proper preparation to sustain the multitude of God's spiritual children. Substantial scriptural references indicate the seven creation days were long, extended periods of time. These long creation days each extended for millions to billions of years. The three scriptural accounts of the creation, Genesis, the book of Moses, and the book of Abraham, provide credible justification for the following conclusions: (1) The creation was a gradual process that occurred step-by-step. (2) Creation started with the introduction of simple organisms and proceeded to the more complex. (3) The Gods carefully planned, organized, and were directly involved with the creation. (4) The Gods utilized and harnessed the natural laws and principles of chemistry and physics to achieve the creation. The creation process determined from modern science is shown to be perfectly consistent with these same four conclusions derived from the scriptures.

For every scriptural creation event described, there are clear and identifiable corresponding parallel details available from science. The similarity between the creation events from the scriptures and science are so striking that approximate dates for the scriptural-based events could be assigned. Latter-day scriptures describe changes in the reckoning of time between our day and that prior to the fall of Adam. Modern science is unlocking clues to how these time changes could have occurred. The scriptures were written thousands of years ago, yet they amazingly resemble the most current scientific facts. The prophetic predictability of the scriptures provides a substantial witness to its divine nature and authenticity.

Bibliography

Einstein, Albert. 1956. *Out of my later years.* Secaucus, N.J.: Citadel Press.

Eyring, Henry. 1983. *Reflections of a scientist.* Ed. H. R. Eyring. Salt Lake City: Deseret Book Co.

Hubble, E. 1929. *National Academy of Sciences Proceedings*, 15:168–73.

Laitman, Jeffrey T., et al. 1996. *Proceedings of the National Academy of Sciences USA*, 93:10543–45.

Morris, Henry, M., and Gary E. Parker. 1987. *What is creation science.* El Cajon, Calif.: Master Books.

Ross, Hugh. 1994. *Creation and time.* Colorado Springs: Navpress.

Ross, Hugh. 1998. *The Genesis question.* Colorado Springs: Navpress.

Schwartz, Jeffrey T., and Ian Tattersall. 1996. *Proceedings of the National Academy of Sciences USA,* 93:10852–54.

Skousen, W. Cleon. 1953. *The first 2,000 years.* Salt Lake City: Bookcraft.

Smith, Joseph Fielding. 1954. *Doctrines of salvation*. Comp. Bruce R. McConkie. Vol. 1. Salt Lake City: Bookcraft.

Smith, Joseph Fielding. 1972. *Teaching of the Prophet Joseph Smith*. Salt Lake City: Deseret Book Co.

Whitfield, Simon I., et al. 1995. *Nature* 378:379–80.

About the Author

David N. Brems was born in Salt Lake City, Utah, in 1951. He served a mission to the Texas South Mission and has been married to Annette Cook for nearly thirty years. The author's greatest accomplishment and challenge has been the raising of their six children. His favorite responsibility is being a grandfather. He is a high priest and has served in a variety of church positions, including elder's quorum president and two bishoprics.

The author received a bachelor's degree in biology and a Ph.D. in biochemistry from the University of Utah. He completed two postdoctoral research fellowships, one at the University of Iowa and the other at Stanford University. Dr. Brems has worked as a scientist in the biopharmaceutical field for almost twenty years. He is currently a Director of Pharmaceutics at Amgen, Inc., in Newbury Park, California, the world's largest biotechnology company. He has published over sixty articles in scientific journals and is the inventor of several patents. Dr. Brems' research area of expertise is in protein structure, function, and engineering.